Irrepressible Light

IRREPRESSIBLE Light

The Women of the New Testament

PATRICIA SHARBAUGH

Paulist Press
New York / Mahwah, NJ

Cover image by EveMax/Shutterstock.com
Cover and book design by Lynn Else

Library of Congress Cataloging-in-Publication Data
Names: Sharbaugh, Patricia, author.
Title: Irrepressible light : the women of the New Testament / Patricia Sharbaugh.
Description: New York : Paulist Press, 2020.
Identifiers: LCCN 2019016738 (print) | LCCN 2019980323 (ebook) | ISBN 9780809153657 (pbk. : alk. paper) | ISBN 9781587687358 (ebook)
Subjects: LCSH: Women in the Bible—Biography. | Jesus Christ—Friends and associates—Biography.
Classification: LCC BS2445 .S53 2020 (print) | LCC BS2445 (ebook) | DDC 225.9/22082—dc23
LC record available at https://lccn.loc.gov/2019016738
LC ebook record available at https://lccn.loc.gov/2019980323

ISBN 978-0-8091-5365-7 (paperback)
ISBN 978-1-58768-735-8 (e-book)

Published by Paulist Press
997 Macarthur Boulevard
Mahwah, New Jersey 07430
www.paulistpress.com

Printed and bound in the
United States of America

To John with all my love,
and with gratitude for the life we have received,
created, loved, lived, and cherished together

Contents

Preface

When I was a teenager, I kept a Bible hidden between the mattress and box spring of my bed. No one in my family would have objected to me having a Bible, so this is not the reason I kept it hidden. I kept it hidden because it was so important to me and, while my family might not object to me having the Bible, if they sensed how important it was to me, they would have teased me about it. They would have ridiculed me for taking it so seriously. Perhaps keeping it hidden was one of my first steps toward wisdom. By hiding it, I protected my love of scripture so that it could find roots within me; hide in deep, dark, good soil until this love was strong enough to make its way toward the light.

Scripture has been my companion as I have journeyed through life. It has been beside me and within me when leaving the bedroom of my youth to go to college, getting married, joining the Catholic Church, having children, attending seminary, earning a PhD in theology, and embarking on a teaching career at St. Vincent College. I teach courses on scripture now and spend hours a day studying its texts, yet I still feel like a beginner.

The pages of scripture open up to manifold paths. These paths allow you to explore who you are and the meaning of your life, lead you to walk in gratitude, help you to find beauty in every moment of life, even moments of sorrow, and open up ways to see that you were unaware of before. Most importantly, scripture tells us that God is very near. Although God is transcendent, God does not reside in some remote region of separation to be guessed at and reasoned about but draws near to us and remains with us. We can experience God in our own lives. God is deep, deep within us, loving us, meeting us, freeing us, guiding us, rejoicing in and with us, part of us. We can learn to see the world through God. We see most clearly as we forgive and love what is most broken in ourselves and others.

My relationship to scripture has not always been an easy one. When I pulled that Bible out from under my mattress and opened its pages, I was attracted to it but confused by it as well. I did not understand it. When I was in high school, I attended a Bible study and I always felt like an outsider. Everyone else seemed to be comforted by the Bible's message and to think that God was making things in their life work out perfectly, but I would read about plucking out eyes, cutting off hands, and being thrown into the outer darkness where there was weeping and gnashing of teeth. Unlike my Bible study companions, I wasn't sure if the Bible's message to me was one of comfort or dismay. I hoped I was living my life in a way that God would accept, but I was not at all sure that I wasn't the one in the dark. I am sure it was my uncertainty that drove my search for deeper answers.

My search for deeper answers led me to wonderful writers and teachers. As a college student, I was introduced to Thomas Merton, and he has been a lifelong companion. As a young mother, I read spirituality books by Madeline L'Engle. These books taught me that God could be found in and through the daily challenges and joys of family life. When I attended Seminary, I had wonderful professors who taught me how to explore the pages of scripture through biblical criticism and inspired me by the quality of their spiritual lives. I have lived my life with the spiritual friendship of many authors of spirituality books: Kathleen Norris, Margaret Guenther, Bonnie Thurston, Esther de Waal, Henri Nouwen, Michael Casey, Joan Chittister, Abraham Heschel, Karl Rahner, Frederick Buechner, and Wendy Wright. Writing this book has been a way to continue my conversations with them. It has been a joyous path of discovery. Weaving my own story into the stories I have read and studied for so many years has helped me to know more clearly truths I only glimpsed before.

This book focuses on New Testament stories about women who encountered Jesus. These women are strong, daring, faithful, and brave. Though they are poor, ill, misunderstood, and oppressed, these women find a way to listen to the dimly burning irrepressible light within. This flicker of dim light calls them forth from their poverty, pain, isolation, and suffering to encounter the healing, saving mystery of God. I have tried to learn from their stories by asking how and why they were able to be so strong, so daring, so faithful, and so brave. I have tried to listen to them so that they might show me their way to know and love God so that I too might find a way to see and follow the irrepressible light within.

I offer this book to you in the spirit of friendship. It is not meant to be definitive, unique, or in any way exceptional. It is my ordinary thoughts about living an everyday, ordinary, spiritual life. I have studied the stories I am writing about. I have read good commentaries and wonderful articles on the passages. For each story, I chose one of many paths of interpretation that might be taken and then I let myself be free and creative. When I talked to my children about my hopes for writing this book, my daughter Rebecca said, "Be brave when you write." I have tried to take her advice. I have tried to bravely write from my own perspective with my own voice, knowing that this perspective and this voice is just one voice among many. My hope is that when you read my thoughts about the biblical text, when you read about how I see my own story in light of scripture, you might also think about what scripture means to you and see your own story interwoven with the biblical story.

I teach a course at St. Vincent College called Catholic-Jewish dialogue. I co-teach this class with a distinguished, well-respected, beloved Rabbi named Jason Edelstein. In class this past semester we discussed a well-known Jewish teaching about Torah. It says, "Turn it [Torah] over and over for everything is in it, and grow old and gray in it, and do not turn away from it, for there is no better rule for you than it (M. Avot 5:35)."[1] Turning the biblical text over and over is necessary because the Bible speaks to us through all the different moments of our lives and through all our various experiences. Its meaning is never exhausted, we will never finish understanding it, but if we keep looking, if we keep trying, we might find a way to let it shape our lives so that it lives in us, with us, and through us.

Acknowledgments

I am grateful for the opportunity to thank all the institutions and people that supported this writing project. I am thankful for the three faculty research grants I received from St. Vincent College. These grants gave me the opportunity to spend my summers writing. I greatly appreciate the encouragement I received from Fr. Rene Kollar, OSB, the Dean of Humanities and Fine Arts at St. Vincent College, and Dr. Jason King, the Chair of the Theology Department. Both Fr. Rene and Dr. King affirmed my decision to turn to spiritual writing in the midst of my academic work, and their encouragement made it possible for me to begin this project. I am so very thankful for my colleagues in the Theology Department, Dr. Jason King, Dr. Christopher McMahon, Fr. Nathan Munsch, OSB, and Dr. Catherine Petrany. Because of you, it is a joy to come to work every day.

While I really only began the physical writing of this manuscript three years ago, my rumination on the spirituality of the women in the New Testament began with a course I took at Pittsburgh Theological Seminary in 1997 taught by Dr. Bonnie Thurston. One of the assignments in the course was to write a biography of a woman in the New Testament. The combination of academic research and creative thought required for that assignment opened within me connections between my imagination and the biblical text. I am grateful to Bonnie for her teaching, writing, and friendship.

I am particularly grateful to the first readers of this manuscript, Catherine Petrany, Rita McKnight, and Molly Sharbaugh. Their thoughtful comments about the writing and our discussions of the material helped me to feel connected to a community as I was writing. My friendship with these three kind, compassionate, thoughtful, and intelligent women brings me deep joy.

I am grateful to Trace Murphy for his enthusiastic response to my manuscript and for giving it a home at Paulist Press. I am also grateful to Donna Crilly for her editing work and to Enrique Aguilar for his generous and reliable communication with me during the editing process.

Finally, all the joyful parts of this manuscript revolve around my husband, children, and grandchildren. My heart overflows with beauty, peace, gentleness, love, and wonder every time I get to spend time with John, Patrick, Christina, Rebecca, Tony, Molly, Jared, Eliza, Sebastian, Rosalie, and Apollo. With them, I know who I am and why I am alive. Through them, I receive God's love. Because of them, my life abounds with meaning, life, light, and joy.

CHAPTER 1

Prodigal Giving

He sat down opposite the treasury, and watched the crowd putting money into the treasury. Many rich people put in large sums. A poor widow came and put in two small copper coins, which are worth a penny. Then he called his disciples and said to them, "Truly I tell you, this poor widow has put in more than all those who are contributing to the treasury. For all of them have contributed out of their abundance; but she out of her poverty has put in everything she had, all she had to live on."

Mark 12:41–44

The possibility of writing a book focused on learning to see with the women in the New Testament began to take root in me during the season of Christmas. At this time I read an essay by Karl Rahner called "Thoughts on the Theology of Christmas." In this essay Rahner says that we don't find the meaning of Christmas in trees, gift-giving, good food, or cozy homes. Rather, we find the meaning of Christmas when we have the courage to be alone, for it is in our solitude that we experience what Christmas teaches: that "God's remoteness is the incomprehensibility of his all-pervading nearness." God is "there like the pure light which, spread over everything, hides itself by making everything else visible in the silent lowliness of its being." Rahner says that Christmas tells us to "trust the nearness, it is not emptiness; let go and then you will find; give up and then you will be rich."[1] Christmas, then, is the celebration of the love of God that is the heart of all we know. God gives himself to us in Christ. Our deepest experience of love is rooted in God's giving of Christ and in our receiving this gift. If we experience in our solitude the truth of God becoming human in Jesus Christ, the incarnation we celebrate at Christmas, we discover that God is so very near to us that we are a mystery to ourselves. We find ourselves by losing ourselves, by orienting ourselves toward something greater, while at the same time finding this something greater through the very center of our deepest and truest selves.

With these thoughts in mind, I was drawn to Mark 12:41–44, the story of the poor widow throwing two small coins into the temple treasury. The story of this woman is fascinating because it has so many layers of meaning. Its placement in the Gospel of Mark suggests that the writer sees her as an ideal disciple of Jesus and a contrast to both the Jewish leaders and the twelve apostles. Her act is praised by Jesus, and yet in the context of Mark, it is a reason for condemnation of the leaders of the temple. Jesus's attentive recognition of her generosity of heart reveals to us God's concern with our smallest actions, actions that go largely unnoticed in the world. All these topics are worth exploring, but the primary questions that emerge for me when I read this story are these: How is the widow able to give from her poverty, from her need? Is it even right for her to give from her need? How does she find her way to this faith? What does her action teach us about drawing close to God?

Mother Teresa of Calcutta tells an incredible story about a woman in Calcutta as generous as this poor widow in Mark. This woman in Calcutta was the mother of several children and was living in poverty, immersed in the suffering that hunger brings. Mother Teresa brought a bag of rice to the one-room dwelling where this mother and her children lived. After thanking Mother Teresa for the gift of rice, the first thing this mother did was to divide the rice in two and take half of the rice to the woman next door, who was also a mother with several children, sharing the same dire circumstances as her neighbor. When Mother Teresa tells this story, she says that what surprised her most was not the generosity of this young mother, but the fact that she knew her neighbor was hungry. When people are trying to survive harsh situations, their world can become very small, their energy is directed toward survival, and it becomes very difficult to see anyone else.

I can't even recall where I read this story many years ago, but it has stayed with me. It is a story that convicts me because I know I would not share that rice with my neighbor. I would justify my lack of sharing with the thought that my own children are my primary responsibility and they need the rice. Mother Teresa's story, like the story of the poor widow in Mark's Gospel, raises the question about whether it is right for a person to give from her poverty, from her need.

The writer of Mark wrestles with this question as well. The placement of the story of the generous widow in the Gospel fills the story with ambiguity. When the story is taken out of context and is read on its own, it unequivocally praises the woman's actions. Furthermore, in the context of Mark, the widow is seen in contrast to the surrounding characters, the scribes and leaders of the synagogue, as one who exemplifies faithfulness and complete devotion to God. She becomes the example for the leaders. The ambiguity comes in, however, when this story is read in its immediate context, following Jesus's condemnation of the scribes for devouring the houses of widows (12:38–40) and before Jesus's announcement that the temple will be destroyed (13:1–2).

In the story immediately preceding the story about the widow, Jesus warns his disciples about certain scribes. These scribes wear fancy clothes and make sure they are seated in the very best and most attention-worthy seats in public. Jesus claims that they "devour widows' houses" while reciting lengthy prayers. These scribes are the powerful in society, the ones with status and respect, the people consulted for their expertise. The statement that they "devour widows' houses" is a profound accusation, especially when viewed through the lens of the Old Testament.

Throughout the Old Testament, widows are often grouped with orphans and aliens because these three groups share common human experiences. They are powerless and therefore the most vulnerable in society. Israel, as a society called to live God's justice and compassion in the world, is to have special concern for the widow, orphan, and alien. In fact, the widow, orphan, and alien provide a test case for Israel. If these vulnerable groups are being taken care of, Israel is living according to the covenant with God. Likewise, if these groups are being oppressed, then Israel is failing to live according to the covenant.[2]

Therefore, when Jesus claims that the scribes devour the houses of widows, this is a statement of condemnation.[3] The hearts of the scribes are revealed in their treatment of the widows. The scribes are experts on the law; they are interpreters and teachers of the law, theologians and guardians of tradition. Despite knowing the law, the scribes Jesus refers to allow poor widows to support their work. While claiming to be for God, these scribes use religion to secure themselves, to secure their own honor, status, and respect. In light of this Old Testament background, the placement of the story of the poor widow's prodigal giving between Jesus's observation of the scribes and his statement about the future destruction of the temple is significant. The writer of Mark's Gospel clearly sees two realities revealed by the widow's prodigal giving. On the one hand, she provides a remarkable example of faith. On the other hand, her giving reveals a community rooted in sin. The ambiguity of Mark's presentation of this story is important for us to observe as we seek to answer the question, Is it even right for the woman to give from her need?

Mark's placement of this story reflects the ambiguity of what it means to be faithful to God amid the reality of the world. The woman's prodigal giving is an expression of her faithfulness. Her giving comes from a heart so filled with the love of God, it can't help but overflow, and yet her giving also reflects her situation in a world of sin. In a perfect world, this woman would not be giving from her poverty, from her need. If Israel was living its calling to be the embodiment of God's love, fidelity, and compassion in the world, this woman would not be in need. She would not be giving the money she needed to care for her basic needs to the temple. Instead, the community called to worship the God of Israel would be making sure her basic needs were met. Despite the failure of her community to show concern for her situation, this widow abandons herself and lives with complete trust in the generosity of God. She shows us what it means to live out of spiritual abundance in a world of need, poverty, and sin.

Before we try to understand how she can give in this way, I think it is important to explore the story at a level deeper than its historical and social context. On the level of historical and social context, the story revolves around issues of wealth and poverty, social status, power, and vulnerability. Understanding the historical and social context of the story is vital to correct interpretation. Its placement in Mark challenges us to work to alleviate oppression and poverty in our communities and in the world. This aspect of the story should not be lost, but I think that the ambiguity of Mark's placement of the story doesn't merely speak to an external social situation. Rather, the story's meaning is deepened and becomes more profound when we recognize that the external ambiguity of its social location reflects an internal ambiguity deeply rooted in our souls. The outward actions of the scribes to secure themselves flow out of a deeply held internal insecurity, an internal insecurity to which I can easily relate.

The scribes have spent their adult lives studying the Bible. They are experts and leaders, but their actions reveal that living according to God's word is much harder than merely knowing what the word commands. Living according to God's word requires us to risk our security, to abandon ourselves to God's generosity, to live in trust, rather than actively seeking to secure ourselves. This is such a hard thing to do! We have not traveled as far as we would like from our early ancestors who hoped to build a tower that reached the heavens in order to secure themselves. Like the builders of that tower, these scribes show us ourselves. The scribes in Mark are not merely historical figures who lived in first-century Palestine and had religious attitudes in contrast to Christianity. It is far too easy for us as Christians to paint Judaism with broad strokes, indicting them with failure to live according to God's promises, projecting our own failures onto them, and walking away with a clear contrast between the problems of Judaism and the promise of Christianity. Instead, we need to admit that these scribes are like us. The insecurity they display is our insecurity. Their attempts to secure themselves resonate with us.

I can easily relate to the scribes. I devote myself to biblical studies. I study interpretation, read the Bible devotionally, teach the Bible academically. I can tell you the literary context for Jesus's words, "For those who want to save their life will lose it, and those who lose their life for my sake, and for the sake of the gospel, will save it" (Mark 8:35), but I have a much harder time living these words. I know I would never be like the generous mother that Mother Teresa encountered in Calcutta. Likewise, I am confident that I would not be like this widow in Mark's story. I know this because I have so much more material security than either of these women, and yet I am inclined even in my material abundance to hold onto things others could use, just in case I might need them down the road. So how can I, a scribe, become more like the widow? How can my need for security be transformed so that I can live a life of spiritual abundance?

I can only begin where I am. While I have never shared the material and social insecurity of the widow in this story, I can identify with her poverty on one level. My poverty, my need, is in the area of self-confidence, self-esteem. I have a very strong, negative, critical voice in my head. This voice was once the only song I heard, and at times in my life, I have wrestled with depression and feelings of despair. I have learned to listen to new tunes, and for the most part, I dance to more optimistic music these days. The strong, negative, critical voice in my head was central to my life for all of my formative years, however, and so despite all the healing my life has brought, the scar tissue of that voice remains and sometimes rips open, exposing the chaotic dark waters that lie below the fresh skin of my healed and healthy self. This ripping open happens most often when I am tired and over-whelmed, and I find it difficult to maneuver my way through the darkness that envelops me at these times. The demands of my life do not stop because I am feeling this way. It is in these times, times when the darkness surrounds me but demands confront me, that I have learned to surrender myself fully to God. I have a choice to give into the darkness and abandon my commitments, or to hand myself over with trust in God's generosity to see me through. I don't try to overcome the darkness. Like bad weather, I accept that I must live through it, but I find that I can still function, still walk into the classroom, into meetings, into whatever situation I am called to enter, having no confidence in myself but trusting that God is with me.

I have even learned to value the darkness because it is in that darkness that I discover deep within myself an irrepressible, dimly burning light allowing me to see the world in a new way. When I am living on the surface of life, untroubled by deeper waters, I am less aware of the dimly burning light within. I can delude myself into believing that I am in control of my life. I am active rather than receptive. I strain to accomplish, working with discipline and determination. I fill the world with my actions, my words, my voice, and my opinions. In the darkness, I discover that I am vulnerable. I am not as much in control of my life as I like to think, and beneath the pretense of control lay chaos, disorder, and insecurity. The only way forward is through trust, releasing my hold, letting myself be taken by the deeper undercurrent of my life that I do not control. But often once I release myself from control of my life, I find that riding the current opens within me a space to receive. I find myself in a quiet place that is comfortably dark, and yet if I listen closely enough, I am able to see this small, unobtrusive light, a light that fills me with energy, passion, and the desire to live more openly. I find that chaos, disorder, and insecurity are not all that lie beneath the pretense of control. Exploring this space, venturing forth as a pilgrim into the unknown, shutting out the warning anxiety that arises in me when I sacrifice control opens a way for me to surrender myself to the mystery of God, whom I believe is both the darkness that surrounds me and the source and energy of this irrepressible light.

> For with you is the fountain of life;
> in your light we see light.
>
> (Ps 36:9)

Furthermore, the more deeply I surrender to this mystery, the more I become aware of deeper and richer aspects of myself, my true self, the self that is gift from God and is found in God.

When, despite darkness, despair, and lack of confidence, I walk into the classroom and give to my students from my poverty, I find a way to understand the sacrifice of the poor widow in Mark. Unlike my small surrender in the most ordinary of circumstances, this widow has little choice in regard to surrender. She does not need times of darkness to help her see her pretense of control; she has no pretense of control. She knows from the roots of her being that she is vulnerable, alone, without control, and without security. And yet she is also free. This woman's giving of two small coins shows that she is not imprisoned by her vulnerability in the world, her lack of social status, her apparent powerlessness. Like the mother in Mother Teresa's story, her eyes are opened to see her connection to others. She understands that she is not the only person to suffer and that she has the power to act freely in the world. She has value; she can give to God by giving to others. Her exterior actions reveal an interior world rooted in security, forged, formed, grounded, and upheld by the prodigal love of God. Through her poverty, in her poverty, this widow found her way to a wealth that cannot be taken. She has come to understand the all-pervading nearness of God. She has learned to live in and from this nearness.

It is remarkable that she doesn't have to leave her poverty behind to find her way to this truth. In fact, her poverty is the path she walks to find this truth. This is an incredibly freeing idea. No matter how dire our circumstances, how deep our poverty, or how strong our feelings of worthlessness, we can give ourselves to God, right now, in this moment. We aren't to wait for the circumstances to be perfect, good, or even better. We give where we are. We give from our need. After all, at Christmas we celebrate God coming into the world as a vulnerable infant not because the world was perfect, or even good, but because God so loved the world. Jesus identifies himself with our need, joins in our poverty, and offers himself to God for us. The last stanza of Thomas Merton's poem *Hagia Sophia* speaks eloquently of Jesus's poverty:

> She [Mary, Sophia] sends the infinitely Rich and Powerful One forth as poor and helpless, in His mission of inexpressible mercy, to die for us on the Cross.
>
> The Shadows fall. The stars appear. The birds begin to sleep. Night embraces the silent half of the earth.
>
> A vagrant, a destitute wanderer with dusty feet, finds his way down a new road. A homeless God, lost in the night, without papers, without identification, without even a number, a frail expendable exile lies down in desolation under the sweet stars of the world and entrusts Himself to sleep.[4]

CHAPTER 2

A Life Shaped to See

There was also a prophet, Anna the daughter of
Phanuel, of the tribe of Asher. She was of a great age,
having lived with her husband seven years after her
marriage, then as a widow to the age of eighty-four.
She never left the temple but worshiped there with
fasting and prayer night and day. At that moment she
came, and began to praise God and to speak about the
child to all who were looking for the redemption of
Jerusalem.

Luke 2:36–38

I competed in the sport of gymnastics for ten years. Gymnastics is a very demanding sport, and even at the age of twelve, I practiced three to four hours a day, six days a week. These practices were characterized by overcoming. We were asked to overcome fear when we tried a new skill. We were asked to overcome the pain of bruised hips and ripped hands from the bars, scrapes, bumps, and contusions from falling on the beam, and sore ankles from landing vaults and tumbling passages wrong. We were asked to overcome our exhaustion and to overcome distractions so we could concentrate at a level beyond our years. After a week of this demanding, daunting discipline, the end of practice on Saturday was welcomed with relief, a sense of freedom, and the joy of simply being twelve. Occasionally on Saturdays, my fellow gymnasts and I would walk into downtown Johnstown to have lunch at McDonald's. I remember these occasions so well, feeling young, joyful, carefree, and at the same time so excited to be "grown up" enough to go to lunch without an adult. It was on one of these Saturdays that I first entered into a Roman Catholic Church.

I am not a cradle Catholic but joined the church twenty-eight years ago when I was pregnant with my first child. My parents belonged to the Presbyterian Church but we rarely attended. I went to church a smattering of times during my childhood and had a vague familiarity with the story of Jesus. There were several girls on my gymnastics team who went to Catholic school. I knew that their faith was very important to them, and I was always envious of the security and identity that their solid grounding in Catholicism brought them.

One Saturday when I was twelve, I walked to lunch with two of my closest friends on the team, Kathy Klug and Linda Kelly. At the beginning of our pilgrimage to McDonald's, we passed the Catholic Church my friend Kathy attended. She turned and asked the two of us if we would like to see the inside of her church. Linda, who was Presbyterian like me, informed us that her mother told her she would go to hell if she went into a Catholic church. I had never heard this idea and wasn't sure what to think about it, but at the time, hell seemed to be a remote threat and the church was right in front of me, so I said I would love to go inside.

As Linda waited for us outside, Kathy and I entered the church. I remember this experience so well. I remember walking behind Kathy and following her actions as she dipped her

hand into the holy water, made the sign of the cross, genu-
flected, and kneeled in the pews. The silence, the dim, flick-
ering light of candles, the statues, and the crucifix enveloped
me and awakened within me a yearning I did not know that I
had. It is an experience I have difficulty describing, a moment
of awakening to a reality that I knew was vitally important
and yet lay beyond my comprehension. As I knelt there and
looked around, I saw three or four old women kneeling in
silent prayer in that dark and empty church. While they were
probably not much older than I am right now, they seemed
very old to me at the time. These women silently praying
have remained with me all my life. I don't know who they are
and they certainly don't remember me, but they were evan-
gelists that day. Their actions witnessed to the depth of their
faith. Without knowing it, they showed me a path I longed to
walk and have been learning to walk ever since. When I read
the story of the prophetess Anna, I think of these women.

The story of Anna comes toward the end of chapter 2
in the Gospel of Luke. These chapters are referred to as the
birth narrative and are centered on stories surrounding the
births of John the Baptist and Jesus. The temple dominates
these early chapters, as does the faithful piety of Zechariah,
Elizabeth, Mary, Simeon, and Anna. The birth narrative is the
beginning of the good news of Jesus Christ, the unfolding of
a new era in salvation history, but the writer of Luke's Gospel is clear that this story can only be understood in light of
Israel's story and with Israel's story as the foundation of all
that is about to unfold.

The birth narrative begins in the temple when Zechariah is chosen by lot to burn incense on the altar within the
Holy Place and is confronted there by the angel Gabriel, who
tells him his wife, Elizabeth, will bear a son. It concludes in
the temple with a story about Jesus, aged twelve, showing
wisdom beyond his years. The temple is featured in one other

story in the birth narrative, the story about Joseph and Mary bringing the infant Jesus to the temple to consecrate him to God. In this story, when the infant Jesus arrives at the temple, his significance is noted by two important figures, Simeon and Anna.

Simeon and Anna have lived a long time: Simeon is ready to die, and Anna is at least eighty-four years old.[1] The length of years they have lived is meant to accentuate the extended time of their attentive, faithful waiting. They are both people of prayer and together seem to represent the faithful of Israel who hoped for and expected God's consolation and redemption of Israel. When Simeon and Anna see the infant Jesus, they both give thanks to God and speak about the child, connecting him to this redemption.

There is a noticeable distinction between Simeon and Anna however. While the writer of Luke's Gospel is careful to record both Simeon's words to God and his words to Mary, Anna's words never appear. Anna is described as a prophetess. She is the only woman designated a prophetess in the Gospels and the only person besides Jesus described in this way by Luke.[2] While prophets are usually associated with speech, identified by the words they proclaim, Anna's words go unreported. Instead, we are told of her background, of her faithful practice in the temple, and finally of her actions after the infant Jesus was brought to the temple. Some biblical scholars note that Luke depicts women in traditional roles and this might be a reason for the unreported speech, but do these missing words play any other role?[3] Do the missing words ask us to focus our attention on Luke's extensive characterization of Anna instead?[4] What does Luke's description of Anna teach us about Anna's spirituality, a spirituality that allowed her to recognize God's redemption in the infant Jesus? What can we learn from Anna's life so that our lives, like hers, might be shaped to see?

First, like my Catholic friends on the gymnastics team, Anna's identity is formed from and rooted in a rich religious tradition. Luke tells us that she is the daughter of Phanuel of the tribe of Asher. The name Phanuel is Greek and means "face of God."[5] The name itself is associated with the prophetic tradition. Prophets such as Jacob, Moses, and Elijah were said to have seen God, face-to-face.[6] Furthermore, Elijah, one of the most recognizable representatives of the prophetic tradition, preached his words to the northern tribe of Asher. Anna's prophecy springs from and is deeply rooted in the past, in a history shaped by stories of encounters with God.

Though Anna's identity springs from a rich religious tradition, it is also shaped through life experience. The writer of Luke reports that she was married for seven years and then a widow until she was eighty-four. We know from this brief statement that she knew love and loss. We don't have any details about the quality of her marriage, whether she had pregnancies, miscarriages, or children, but we do know that she spent a period of her life connected to her husband and to the community around her. It is likely that through these connections she knew friendship, joy, love, sadness, fear, anxiety, and loneliness, the whole range of human experiences.

Finally, we are told that her life was shaped by asceticism. Luke tells us that she is continuously in the temple and her time in the temple is marked both night and day by worship, fasting, and prayer. It is from this place of worship, fasting, and prayer that Anna steps into her prophetic role, seeing God face-to-face in the baby Jesus and speaking of this experience to everyone she meets.

Luke records all these steps in Anna's life. He doesn't begin with her asceticism in the temple, but with her religious heritage. He doesn't jump from this heritage to her asceticism in the temple, but carefully includes her marriage and widowhood. It is the whole of her life experience that shapes her seeing. We aren't told many of the details of that life experience, but if we are attentive to what Luke tells us, a clear image of Anna begins to emerge.

I can see her in my mind's eye because I have known people like her. Her physical appearance is not as distinct for me as the quality of her presence. Every gesture she makes testifies to the depths of her wisdom and the rich quality of her life. Her movements are slow, deliberate, and calm, and though she is old, she exudes youth and hospitality. She is curious, open, and interested in others. She creates a welcoming space around her so that people are drawn to her and trust her with the secrets of their hearts. She radiates joy. This joy is not merely surface happiness but is deeply rooted in a life-tested hope that knows suffering and yet perceives that life is sheer gift and recognizes every breath as a connection to both the source of this gift and all other living beings. Every aspect, every step of her life has contributed to the quality of her presence.

While the deep prophetic wisdom of Anna is not the result of any isolated aspect of her life, her ascetic practice in the temple profoundly contributed to her recognition of God's face in the face of Jesus, and is both the most difficult and the most important aspect of her life to grasp. Ascetic practice is a vital component of spiritual life and yet is so easily distorted and misunderstood. When I think about asceticism, I am filled with images of great feats of overcoming: overcoming the distraction of hunger through fasting; overcoming anxiety, need, and loneliness through extended times of isolation in desert climates; overcoming human limitations through the denial of sleep; and overcoming sinfulness through hours spent kneeling in prayer. This emphasis on overcoming fills me with anxiety and stirs my competitive juices as I find myself remembering my long hours of overcoming in the gym. All I can think in the face of these memories is "Run! Run as fast as you can! Asceticism is not for you!" When I link the asceticism of spiritual life to the discipline I learned in the gym, however, I think I am misunderstanding and distorting the role asceticism should play in spiritual life.

Asceticism should not be understood as a way to overcome the limitations of our humanity or to punish ourselves for those limitations. Nor should it be a practice entered into in order to achieve a goal or to accomplish a noteworthy human feat. Instead, asceticism is a way to make space in our lives for our awakening to grace. Rather than overcoming our human limitations, we enter more fully into them because it is in and through these very limitations that we become aware of the beauty of our vulnerability. Through our vulnerability, we recognize our dependence on God and receive our lives as gift. Ascetic discipline in the spiritual life helps us to let go of our illusion of control. It is less about overcoming and more about learning to receive. It is not about achieving, but about moving aside, allowing ourselves to be pushed off-center to make space for God and for others.

Perhaps the best way to understand asceticism is to think of an example we can relate to. There are great, noteworthy ascetics in the Christian tradition like St. Anthony, St. Benedict, and St. Francis. I wish I could relate to them, but the truth is I find their lives and the times in which they lived too far removed from mine to really help me navigate my way through my own life. I relate much better to ordinary ascetics, people I have known who have been shaped by living a long and purposeful life, people like my neighbor Anthony McCarty, who recently passed away at the age of ninety-five.

Mr. McCarty, as I called him, was in many ways a very ordinary man. He served in the Air Force, worked for Sun Oil, played the violin, was married for sixty-seven years, and was a father and grandfather. His asceticism was the asceticism of ordinary life. He didn't seek out opportunities to deny himself but chose denial when his tasks and responsibilities required this of him. His love for music inspired him to cultivate the discipline necessary to be able to play the violin beautifully. His love of music introduced him to his wife— they met when they both played in a symphony in West Virginia—and this same love of music connected him to the wider community. He taught violin to neighborhood children and organized symphonies in his church and in the communities in which he lived right up until the day he died.

I first met Mr. McCarty because he agreed to teach my son Patrick to play the violin. Patrick was only six at the time, and so I would walk with him down our street to the music room in the McCarty house where I would watch Mr. McCarty give a violin lesson to Patrick, a lesson for which he would charge me a mere five dollars. There was a palpable peace and a sacramental sense of the time I spent in that room. I watched as Mr. McCarty taught Patrick to hold his bow, place his fingers on the strings, and read the notes on a staff, but these skills were only the surface manifestations of deeper lessons, lessons about reverence for life, lessons about the way a wise life requires discipline, respect, creativity, beauty, music, and meaning. Mr. McCarty did not convey these deeper lessons with words but with his gentle, patient manner, with his understated delight when Patrick would learn a new piece, and with his interested inquiry to me about how my week had gone. In his quiet, humble way, he communicated wisdom and the rich quality of life he had awakened to over many years of discipline and dedication to his joys and responsibilities.

When he died, my husband, John, and I attended his funeral. It was a bittersweet occasion as his wife, his children, his grandchildren, his friends, and the many people in the community he had touched gathered to celebrate the wonderful long life he had lived. His funeral began with a trio of accomplished violinists playing classical pieces in his memory. As this beautiful music played, I read through the funeral program and noticed that a soloist would be featured during the service. I didn't recognize the name of this soloist and thought she must be quite talented to take this featured role at the funeral of such an accomplished musician. When the time came for this soloist to play, she stood up and her music stand was carried down to the front of the church by her mother. She was eight years old and was Mr. McCarty's most recent student. Her violin had tape marks near the strings to remind her where to place her fingers to form the notes of the two simple songs she played, the same tape marks I remembered Mr. McCarty placing on Patrick's violin years earlier. It was a fitting tribute to a man whose life of ascetic discipline sprang from love. His love for music ran so deep it was contagious. The asceticism of Mr. McCarty was not an asceticism of denial but asceticism in the service of expressing most fully his love for music. He understood that his musical talent was a gift from God and a path for serving God, and he wholeheartedly embraced this gift, giving himself over to it daily for over ninety years. Because the goal of his ascetic practice was not to overcome limitation or weakness but to most fully express his love, his dedicated, disciplined life overflowed to others. His lifelong practice of dedication to his love for music made space for others to experience this same love. The young soloist bravely playing at his funeral was the last of a long line of students who Mr. McCarty had invited into the space his asceticism had made for love.

Hearts shaped by faithful asceticism make room for others. Anna entered into her ascetic practice in the temple after a long life of experiencing God's love through her ancestors, her husband, and her community. Her experience of God's love stirred in her a yearning to see and know God more clearly, to look at God's face. Her lifetime practice of ascetic waiting and hoping shaped her to see God's redemptive, loving face in the face of an infant brought to the temple by his parents. As readers of Luke's Gospel, we aren't told the words that Anna said after she saw Jesus, but we are shown the way her life was shaped to see.

Anna is the great, great, great, great, great, great (who knows how many greats!) grandmother of the women I saw praying in a church in downtown Johnstown one Saturday many years ago. Like her, they testified by their actions to their love for God and opened in my heart the awareness of my own yearning for that love. I have journeyed far from that Saturday when I first stepped into a Roman Catholic church. Much of my journey has been about letting go of overcoming and learning to enter into my human limitations, allowing my vulnerability to be the place I learn to receive. It is a path I am still learning to walk.

CHAPTER 3

Expecting the Unexpected

In those days Mary set out and went with haste to a
Judean town in the hill country, where she entered
the house of Zechariah and greeted Elizabeth. When
Elizabeth heard Mary's greeting, the child leaped in her
womb. And Elizabeth was filled with the Holy Spirit
and exclaimed with a loud cry, "Blessed are you among
women, and blessed is the fruit of your womb. And
why has this happened to me, that the mother of my
Lord comes to me? For as soon as I heard the sound
of your greeting, the child in my womb leaped for joy.
And blessed is she who believed that there would be a
fulfillment of what was spoken to her by the Lord."

Luke 1:39–45

Babies shake up our worlds. Ask anyone. Even in the very
best of circumstances, when a baby is longed for, desired,
and born into a welcoming home, a baby carries with it
something that is unexpected, a whole new experience of
life that cannot be explained or understood outside of that
experience. No matter how many books expectant parents

read, how long they wait, how much they prepare, the reality of a baby, the reality of parenthood cannot be fully anticipated.

My daughter Molly has a friend named Violet. When Violet was getting married, she said to Molly, "I can't wait to have a baby so that I can experience this love that is like no other love." Violet was referring to what she had heard all her life about becoming a mother. It is not entirely true that the love a mother experiences is wholly different from every other kind of love. In fact, love comes to everyone in many different ways and every experience of love teaches us something about its nature. And yet, lying at the heart of Violet's statement is the truth that love is what parenthood is all about. We know that babies bring with them uncertainty, sleepless nights, worries, messy diapers, less freedom, the need to leave the house with bags full of supplies, great expenses, a lifetime of commitment, and many other difficult and challenging issues, and yet the announcement of a pregnancy is usually met with great joy, hope, and celebration. We are willing to accept all of the demands and responsibilities a baby brings because somewhere in our deepest wisdom, we know that a baby is sacramental. A baby has the power to open us up to a love so true and deep that it connects us to all other love and reveals for us something of the mystery of love that is the source of all we know. But as much as we might hope for, desire, and want a baby, there is always something chaotic and unexpected about a baby's arrival.

This is one of the most beautiful aspects of Luke's birth narrative found in the first two chapters of the Gospel. Despite weighty pronouncements of the destiny of Jesus and hymns sung about his future as the future of Israel, woven throughout this narrative are unexpected and often chaotic moments. There are unexpected announcements of forthcoming births followed by unexpected pregnancies, pregnancies that came later than hoped for, and those that came earlier than desired. There is the chaotic moment of labor and birth in a stable far from home. There are unlikely messengers, shepherds coming from their fields, and an old widow in the temple. These stories are filled with great promise and hope but never lose the thread of unexpected turmoil that testifies to the reality of incarnation. The story of the one who will shake up the world begins by shaking up the worlds of two particular mothers, Elizabeth and Mary. Their stories, stories about their own experiences of becoming mothers, have a great deal to teach us about the nature of love.

The story of Mary visiting Elizabeth in the hill country of Judea lies in the eye of the storm. A calm and quiet moment, it comes after the announcements of her unexpected pregnancy, and before the tension-filled moment of the birth of Jesus. This moment shared between Elizabeth and Mary is precious because even though the births of John the Baptist and Jesus have implications for all of Israel, in fact for the world, this story, this moment is a simple, personal, private encounter between two expectant mothers, an encounter of intimacy shared between two women who love each other. I want to start here, in this moment of quiet encounter, to begin to think about what we might learn from Elizabeth and Mary, because most of the lessons of motherhood come in quiet, private, intimate moments. These moments are not the kind of moments reported by news anchors or historians, nor are they moments that earn money, fame, or esteem in the world. But in these moments, the quiet pulse of life can be felt.

I remember one of these moments outside in my backyard. My daughter Molly was about a year old. It was spring. I was just sitting beside her as she stood at a small stone wall that runs across our backyard. Her hands were on top of the wall and she suddenly turned her face toward the wind and smiled as the wind swept over her, blowing her hair around her sweet baby face. Molly's discovery of wind became my awakening to movements in the world that have nothing to do with merit, with purpose, with earning respect, but have everything to do with living a spiritual life, with waiting for a glimpse of the gentle love that animates the world.

Elizabeth glimpses the gentle love that animates the world when she feels the baby in her womb leap for joy at the sound of Mary's greeting. In a small movement only she can feel, she knows that God has drawn very near. Furthermore, her child has led her to recognize the unexpected. Just as Jacob and Esau's wrestling in Rebekah's womb led Rebekah to know unexpectedly that "the older will serve the younger," so also the leaping in Elizabeth's womb leads her to the unexpected recognition that the child in Mary's womb is her Lord. Elizabeth responds to this moment of recognition with declarations of blessing. She recognizes in Mary the same faith she herself has exhibited, an open, complete trust in God that takes refuge in God even in the face of the unexpected.

Elizabeth and Mary both receive God's gift of life. They receive it without condition. Despite unexpected pregnancies, unexpected messengers, and even glimpses of sorrow to come in their future, they hold the promises of God in their hearts and don't allow the darkness of anxiety to overshadow the light. They listen to God's heartbeat in angels, shepherds, an old widow, and even in their children's movements. Elizabeth listens to the movement in her womb, and Mary will listen to her twelve-year-old child Jesus when he is first lost and then found in the temple. What they hear is not expected, but then again what could be more unexpected than the incarnation? What could be more unexpected than God entering into the vulnerability of life, joining us in this journey through a transitory, ambiguous world, becoming "obedient to the point of death—even death on a cross" (Phil 2:8). In Elizabeth and Mary's acceptance of the unexpected and their faithfulness as mothers, we can glimpse God's love for us, for God's love is a motherly love.

In a statement attributed to Mother Teresa, the motherly love of God shines through:

> In the silence of the heart God speaks. What does God say? He says: "I have called you by name, you are mine; water will not drown you. I will give up nations for you, you are precious to me, I love you. Even if a mother forgets her child, I will not forget you. I have carved you in the palm of my hand."

Mother Teresa may have said these words, but she is quoting Isaiah, stitching together verses that can be found in Isaiah, chapters 43—49. In these chapters, God's inability to forget Israel is described using the metaphor of a nursing mother. "Can a woman forget her nursing child, or show no compassion for the child of her womb?" (Isa 49:15). If a nursing mother is away from her child, she will be in pain. Her breasts will ache with the fullness of the milk she has produced for her missing child. Isaiah uses this powerful image to comfort Israel while they are in exile in Babylon, a time when their circumstances might have convinced them that God had forgotten them. Instead, Isaiah insists that God's bond to Israel is one that will not allow God to forget them; God will seek them out and find them, bring them back to their land.

This biblical metaphor depicting God as a mother who will suffer pain rather than abandon the child of her womb is continued in the Jewish tradition through a postbiblical female symbol for God referred to as the Shekinah. The word *Shekinah* derives from the Hebrew word *shakan*, which means to dwell. In the Book of Exodus, God dwells with the people (Exod 25:8; 29:45–46).[1] In addition, God descends, overshadows, and leads the people of Israel through symbols like the cloud, fire, and radiant light. In rabbinic teaching, the Shekinah increasingly comes to be associated with God's presence accompanying Israel in unexpected ways in the midst of the broken world. "Come and see how beloved are the Israelites before God, for wither so ever they journeyed in their captivity the Shekinah journeyed with them."[2] Because the Shekinah is associated with God's accompaniment of Israel in the midst of a broken world, the Shekinah also becomes associated with God's compassion, a compassion that suffers with and for those who are suffering. The Mishnah, the first written account of Jewish oral tradition, says this about the Shekinah, "When a human being suffers what does the Shekinah say? My head is too heavy for Me; My arm is too heavy for Me. And if God is so grieved over the blood of the wicked that is shed, how much more so over the blood of the righteous."[3]

Jewish reflections on the Shekinah emphasize God's unexpected presence and deep compassion with and for people in every experience of life. There is no place in the world that is too hostile for the Shekinah. No matter how far away people wander, despite suffering, even at times when people might suspect that God has abandoned them, the Shekinah is present, a seeking, finding, compassionate love, a motherly love that will not forget her child. The Shekinah goes wherever Israel leads, even when Israel is wrong, even when Israel is suffering exile because of her sins.[4]

Christians believe God's loving presence entered into the midst of a broken world through the incarnation. Interestingly, like later Jewish reflections on the Shekinah, John's Gospel describes the incarnation in terms of dwelling, "And the Word became flesh and lived among us" (John 1:14). God's love is experienced face-to-face in Jesus Christ, who pitches his tent in our midst, comes to where we are, and is present amid our broken world, suffering with all who suffer, and healing us through his presence.

It is difficult for us to understand this kind of love. We think that God's love will come to us if we do the right thing, attend Mass the right number of times, say the right words when we pray, and try to be the person God intends for us to be. Even when we understand that God's love is not earned, is not given to us because we merit that love, we are still tempted to think it depends upon our faith. When life begins to overwhelm us, when we find ourselves drowning under the weight of pressures we seem unable to rise above, when we find it hard to catch our breath, we begin to worry that we have lost our faith, or that our faith is not deep enough to sustain us. When we don't understand the depths of God's motherly love, feelings of anxiety and fear prevail because we recognize that if it were entirely up to us to be faithful, if it were entirely up to us to work, or love our way into salvation, we would fail miserably. While our anxiety and fear point us toward the truth of our total dependence on God, at the same time, this anxiety and fear arise because we don't recognize the depths of God's love for us. God, who created us and sustains us, loves us and will never let us go.

There is a children's book written to address a fear children have, that as they begin to move about independently, grow, and develop their own interests, they might find themselves outside of their mother's love and care. *The Runaway Bunny*, by Margaret Wise Brown, tells the story of a baby bunny who says to his mother, "I am going to run away." The baby bunny imagines different ways that he might run away, such as becoming a fish and swimming away. The mother replies, "If you become a fish in a trout stream, I will become a fisherman and I will fish for you." The bunny says, "If you become a fisherman, I will become a rock on the mountain high above you." The mother replies, "If you become a rock on the mountain high above me, I will become a mountain climber and I will climb to where you are." The story continues as the bunny proposes different scenarios and the mother continually convinces the bunny that wherever the bunny goes, she will come and she will find him.[5]

This children's book confronts a fear we never entirely outgrow. Several years ago, I went with our parish priest to visit a sixty-five-year-old man who was dying of cancer. We sat with this man and he shared stories with us of all the important events of his life. The time when he met his wife, when his son was born, the way in which music moved him, and the adventure he had writing a history book that was never quite finished. He talked about the importance of his faith in Jesus Christ, what that faith meant to him and how that faith had shaped his life. And then he paused, and he said, "I guess people keep their faith right up to the end don't they?" Fr. Tom convinced him that indeed people keep their faith right up to death, through death, and into life on the other side. The man's wife, who had been silent up until this time, said to us, "Daniel is afraid he is going to lose his faith. He is afraid that the pain and the lonely walk through cancer into death is going to erode his ability to believe." This man was afraid that he would run away. He knew his total dependence on God, and he knew his own ability to turn away. He was afraid that in the weakness of sickness he would run away and be lost and then find himself abandoned by God. But reflecting on the motherly love of God tells us that he had it wrong. He had it backward. The most important thing was not that Daniel loved God, but that God first loved him. God had a passionate love for Daniel and God was not going to let him go.

One of Pope John Paul II's favorite theologians was Hans Urs von Balthasar. Reflecting on the nature of God's love, Balthasar claimed that there is such freedom in God's love that God even wants to be surpassed and surprised by the beloved.[6] I once casually mentioned Balthasar's thought about God's love in a women's study group at my church and was surprised by the hostile response I received. The women gathered thought that this idea conflicted with their under-standing of God and said things like, "How could I possibly surpass or surprise God? Impossible!!!!" They might be right, but my experience as a mother helps me to make some sense of Balthasar's statement.

When I think of my children, I am proud of their accom-plishments, the things they have done in life that have made them successful and earned them recognition, but these are not the things I will recall if you ask me about my love for them. When I reflect on my love for them, I remember the ways they surprise me. I love that my son, who is a talented, respected software engineer, winds my yarn into balls that have faces on them and leaves them for me to find. I love that my beautiful, intelligent daughter Rebecca can't find her way to the simplest locations, gets lost in her thoughts, and is so kind and thoughtful that she can't take the last Rice Krispie treat from the box but must leave it for somebody else. I love that when my generous, bighearted daughter Molly was in middle school, she told me that she wished we were the same age so that we could be best friends. Through parenting I have learned that what I love in my children is often what is most unexpected, things that cannot be measured, expres-sions of love that can only come from them, things I discover in quiet, private, intimate moments.

So that brings me back to the quiet, intimate moment that Elizabeth and Mary share in the hill country of Judea. . Elizabeth praises Mary for her faithfulness, but both women help us to learn to see through the eyes of faith. At first glance, their faith may look easy because it is calm, quiet, and accepting.

Yet we know that this faith is not a faith that is grasped in one moment, but has to be lived out through many years of waiting, of pondering things in their hearts, in the face of events they do not control, events that do not turn out the way they desire. They open their hearts and hand themselves over to children that come to them in unexpected births and leave them through tragic deaths. Their stories as mothers are filled with great promise and tremendous contradiction. The savior of the world, a child who comes with the assurance that his kingdom will never end, is born in a stable and dies on a cross. His mother's heart sings of great hope and is pierced with sorrow. Elizabeth and Mary's faith is one that knows that trusting in God does not bring them security, it is the security. What they desire matches what they receive, God's all-pervading nearness, awareness that their refuge is the motherly presence of God. Their blessing does not lie in attachment to a particular outcome, but in commitment to the God who draws near to them through all the unexpected joys and sorrows of their lives. They have learned to sing with the Psalmist,

> O LORD, my heart is not lifted up;
>   my eyes are not raised too high;
> I do not occupy myself with things
>   too great and too marvelous for me.
> But I have calmed and quieted my soul,
>   like a weaned child with its mother;
>   my soul is like the weaned child that is
>   with me.
>
> O Israel, hope in the LORD
>   from this time on and forevermore.
>   (Ps 131)

CHAPTER 4

Hoping against Hope

Now there was a woman who had been suffering from hemorrhages for twelve years. She had endured much under many physicians, and had spent all that she had; and she was no better, but rather grew worse. She had heard about Jesus, and came up behind him in the crowd and touched his cloak, for she said, "If I but touch his clothes, I will be made well." Immediately her hemorrhage stopped; and she felt in her body that she was healed of her disease. Immediately aware that power had gone forth from him, Jesus turned about in the crowd and said, "Who touched my clothes?" And his disciples said to him, "You see the crowd pressing in on you; how can you say, 'Who touched me?'" He looked all around to see who had done it. But the woman, knowing what had happened to her, came in fear and trembling, fell down before him, and told him the whole truth. He said to her "Daughter, your faith has made you well; go in peace, and be healed of your disease."

Mark 5:25–34

One reading habit I have cultivated over the years is to record passages I find particularly meaningful in a book I refer to as my quote book. Years ago, moved by the writing of liberation theologian Leonardo Boff, I recorded a few of his sentences in my quote book, which I find provide a wonderful entryway into reflection on the story of the woman with the hemorrhage:

> The Spirit appears as existence, rising above all hatred, hoping against all hope. The Spirit is that little flicker of fire burning at the bottom of the woodpile. More rubbish is piled on, rain puts out the flame, wind blows the smoke away. But underneath everything a brand still burns on, unquenchable….The Spirit sustains the feeble breath of life in the empire of death.[1]

These sentences can only be written by someone acquainted with suffering. Not the kind of suffering that merely flits across the surfaces of a life, not suffering as a temporary condition, but the suffering that occurs when all of life seems to be lived in the shadow of forces that threaten to extinguish life at any and every moment. And yet, despite familiarity with incessant despair, the writer speaks paradoxically of a tenacious hidden hope waiting in the shadows to be fanned into flame, a beautiful silken thread of hope that burns on against all odds, cannot be quenched, and urges and pushes toward life. These few sentences by Boff hold together the two forces that powerfully shape the life of the woman with the hemorrhage, the power of suffering that points toward her death, and the power of the Spirit that inspires her to make her way through a crowd with only a thin, dimly burning hope that perhaps maybe she might still be able to find a way to life.

The meeting of these two forces in the life of the woman with the hemorrhage is clearly expressed in the first few verses of the text. Her story opens with a description of the woman. This description, though brief, reveals a long journey of suffering, isolation, and vulnerability. The arduous journey this woman has endured is made more sharply apparent through Mark's placement of her story. Her story interrupts and is told in the midst of another story, the story of Jairus's daughter. The stories are meant to be read and interpreted together, and when they are read with this in mind, the meaning of each story is deepened through the other. Like the story about the woman with the hemorrhage, the story of Jairus's daughter begins with a description of Jairus. By intertwining these two stories, a clear contrast between the status of Jairus and the vulnerability of the woman is intentionally painted.[2]

Mark's description of Jairus revolves around his status. He is a man with a solid basis of security in his society. Before we are even told his name, we are told that he is a leader, a synagogue official. We know that he has a family and enough money to own and run a large enough household that people from his house come to tell him that his daughter has died. Jairus shows great respect for Jesus, coming before him and falling to his knees to make his request, but it is important to notice that he approaches Jesus from the front and makes a direct request of Jesus to come and heal his daughter.

The description of Jairus provides a clear contrast to the description of the woman with the hemorrhage. While the story of Jairus tells us about his status, his security in society, the story of the woman tells us of her suffering, isolation, and her vulnerability, springing from her marginal status in society. She is a woman in a patriarchal society, with no recorded name, and no apparent relationships. Some biblical women are identified as the mother, daughter, or wife of someone, but she is only identified by her disease, a hemorrhage. We aren't told exactly what this hemorrhage is, but it is likely that it is related to menstrual bleeding, which would make this woman subject to the menstrual purity laws of the holiness code in Leviticus:

> If a woman has a discharge of blood for many days, not at the time of her impurity, or if she has a discharge beyond the time of her impurity, all the days of the discharge she shall continue in uncleanness; as in the days of her impurity, she shall be unclean. Every bed on which she lies during all the days of her discharge shall be treated as the bed of her impurity; and everything on which she sits shall be unclean, as in the uncleanness of her impurity. Whoever touches these things shall be unclean, and shall wash his clothes, and bathe in water, and be unclean until the evening. (15:25–27)

The purity laws of Leviticus, chapter 15, deal with ritual purity and are difficult for us to fully appreciate. It is also difficult to know how much these laws would have affected the woman in a local village with no access to the temple, but even if we are unable to fully appreciate the issue of ritual purity and even if it is unclear how much these laws would affect a woman in a small local community, it is not difficult to imagine that her knowledge of the laws would increase her feeling of alienation by her disease and further isolate her from her community.[3] In addition, she has no money, having spent all her money on doctors, in whose care she has only grown worse. This woman suffers from disease, from poverty, from isolation, and from loneliness. Her physical, mental, and emotional suffering are weighed down by her marginal status in society, and it is not difficult to understand why, unlike Jairus, she approaches Jesus from behind, through a crowd, hoping only to touch his cloak unnoticed. As she approaches Jesus, she says to herself, "If I but touch his clothes, I will be made well." Rarely in the New Testament is an internal dialogue recorded.[4] Because it is unusual, this woman's internal dialogue is a solid place to puzzle over the text. Why is this dialogue included? What does it tell us? How does it help us to understand the story?

Some scholars argue that her internal dialogue reveals an inadequate faith. They point to her belief that just by touching the cloak of Jesus she will be cured as a desire for magic rather than an expression of authentic faith.[5] The problem with this argument though, is that after Jesus cures her, he says, "Daughter, your faith has made you well." There is no indication in the story that her faith is inadequate. Rather than revealing an inadequate faith, I think her internal dialogue plays an entirely different role. I think it invites us to think about the nature of hope and the dynamic interplay of hope and suffering.

There is a character in Victor Hugo's book *Les Misérables* named Fantine. Like the woman with the hemorrhage, Fantine endures great suffering in her life and her suffering is exacerbated by her marginal status in society. Living in eighteenth-century France, Fantine has a child out of wedlock. When this is discovered, she loses her job working in a factory, and with that loss, her ability to support her daughter. Because her condition is judged as immoral by her society, there are no social structures in place to help her. She is forced to try to make ends meet by first selling her hair, then her teeth, and eventually her body as a prostitute. Her mind is always desperately focused on the welfare of her daughter.

After writing of Fantine's sufferings and humiliations for many pages, Hugo writes,

> Life and social order have spoken their last word to her. All that can happen to her has happened. She has endured all, borne all, experienced all, suffered all, lost all, wept for all. She is resigned, with that resignation that resembles indifference as death resembles sleep. She shuns nothing now. She fears nothing now. Every cloud falls upon her, and all the ocean sweeps over her! What matters it to her! The sponge is already drenched.
>
> She believed so at least, but it is a mistake to imagine that man can exhaust his destiny, or can reach the bottom of anything whatever.[6]

Through this description of Fantine, Hugo narrates the interplay of hope and suffering in Fantine's life. On a surface level her profound suffering seems to have made her indifferent, resigned to let life sweep over her with no resistance whatsoever. Her suffering has perhaps even convinced her that she has reached the bottom, that she can somehow find rest in the misery of her acquiescence. It is not that simple, however, because as Hugo states, it is a mistake to imagine that a human being can exhaust her destiny. There is always more and when there is more, there is hope. What is interesting is that this hope does not bring joy for Fantine, but instead increases suffering. If Fantine could actually reach the bottom, if there actually were no more, nothing left for her to do or hope for, she could be fully resigned and let go of all resistance. But she can't reach that bottom, and the little bit of hope that lives under the weight of all her suffering provides just enough light to illuminate all the pain in her darkness.

Jürgen Moltmann, an important theologian of the twentieth century, describes his theological breakthrough as an awakening to the mystery of the interplay of suffering and hope. Having grown up in a German home steeped in German secular philosophy, Moltmann was first introduced to God as a prisoner in a prisoner-of-war camp when an American pastor gave him a Bible. Moltmann talks about how his encounter with the Bible fed his imagination and emotional need. He experienced despair but also a powerful encounter with God that renewed his hope. God became for him a God who can be found behind barbed wire and is present with the broken-hearted. This experience left him with the insight that suffering and hope reinforce one another. The mystery of God and the mystery of suffering are contemplated together. In contemplating suffering, God can be found; and contemplation of God leads one to become sensitive to questions of suffering.[7]

This insight is important as we explore the story about the woman with the hemorrhage. Jesus's healing of this woman is not to be read as a miracle that provides evidence of Jesus's divinity. Rather, the healing points to how we are to understand the divinity of Jesus as revelation of the mercy of God that meets us, accepts us, and heals us where we are, and in whatever form of isolation and alienation that shapes our arrival. The woman's faith is not inadequate because she wants a cure that leans in the direction of magic; instead she wants a cure that leans in the direction of magic because her hope has been shaped by profound suffering. Her suffering has limited her vision of hope and yet, somehow despite all that she has suffered, this woman has hope. Her hope arises from a deep well within, from the little ember of light burning at the bottom of the wood pile, from the core of her being that knows she has value despite the reality of her disease, the reality of her poverty, and the reality of her social marginalization. Somehow enough hope emerges from her deepest self to convince her to defy social convention, sneak up behind Jesus, and touch his cloak.

Even though hope animates her actions, my guess is that this hope was buried too deeply beneath layers of vulnerability, fear, isolation, and loneliness for her to experience it as hope. She was pushed too far down to feel the power of acting on her own behalf, the power of her own agency. Rather, she experienced her movement of hope as a desperate attempt to move away from the oppressive weight of illness and marginalization that surrounded her and threatened to overcome her life.

While I have never experienced the deeply oppressive, overwhelming isolation this woman has experienced, I do remember a time in my life when I too broke the rules out of desperation. At the time, I was sure that my breaking of rules sprang from weakness of character and mendacity. Only later, because someone met my story with compassion, was I able to see that while my actions were not exactly courageous, they were rooted in the deep desire to protect myself at a time when I had very limited resources.

I was in seventh or eighth grade, twelve or thirteen years old. It was in my first years of intense competition in gymnastics. My coach, Mr. Turner, and my mother were heavily invested in my performance. I showed a lot of promise as a gymnast and they both thought the best way to help me to rise to the highest levels of competition in the sport was to push me to be my best at all times. Mr. Turner and my mother had very intense personalities. They were passionate and volatile. My mother often yelled and when she yelled her speech was laced with hurtful insults that cut right through me. At other times, her passion was expressed through angry, guilt-inducing withdrawal and cold silence. Mr. Turner yelled and screamed so often that we gymnasts kept a secret small chalk chart that tracked the levels of his anger on a wall near where we began our run to the vault. The levels of his anger were determined by how red his face turned. When his earlobes began to turn red, we knew that was a signal of concern. Red earlobes often meant that he would begin to throw things. Sometimes it was his clipboard, sometimes shoes, sometimes us. He would sometimes intentionally let me fall when he was supposed to spot me or catch me during a trick and throw me a little bit roughly to the ground. I was afraid of both Mr. Turner and my mother and constantly felt that I could not please either one. The fact that they did not get along with each other and often fought only added to the difficulty I had in negotiating my relationship with each of them.

My best event in gymnastics was the balance beam. This was true at this early stage in my career and remained true until I stopped competing. One skill I mastered early was a front aerial on the balance beam. This trick is simply a front walkover with no hands. I am very flexible, and the skill came easily to me. Back then, the balance beams were not padded, carpeted, or springy, but made of wood. Even though I mastered the skill early, I still had some fairly serious falls resulting in painful bruises and scrapes. After experiencing a number of these falls, I developed a healthy fear of the front aerial on the balance beam.

The gym I attended at this time was in a very old building in downtown Johnstown. The main gym area had once been a theater, and because it was built for this purpose, it was not big enough for all the gymnastics equipment. For this reason, the balance beams were upstairs in a room we referred to as the beam room. You could not see this room from the rest of the gym. During practices, we were split into groups, and we rotated events, so that we practiced all four events over the course of three hours. We usually had more than one coach in the gym at a time. One of our coaches was Mr. Turner's wife, whom we called Sharon. Sharon was kind and a much gentler person than either Mr. Turner or my mother.

The layout of the gym began to affect my performance in an unusual way. When Mr. Turner was upstairs in the beam room, I was able to do my front aerial on the beam with no hesitation, but when he was not in the room and only Sharon was there, my fear of the trick would get the best of me and I would be unable to do this trick. The reason for this is simple. I was afraid of the front aerial, but I was much more afraid of Mr. Turner than I was of the trick, and so it was easy for me to do the trick when he was in the room. I wanted to do the trick when Sharon was there as well, but I just couldn't overcome my fear of the trick when she was the only one in the room. Sharon began to feel disrespected by me and reported my failure to do the front aerial to Mr. Turner. He called me into his office and told me that if I did not manage to do the front aerial when only Sharon was in the beam room, he would not allow me to do the trick in the upcoming meet later that week. Despite my meeting with Mr. Turner, I was still unable to do the trick for Sharon, so when we traveled several hours to our meet later that week, I was not allowed to do the front aerial in my routine.

I performed very poorly in that meet. I don't remember all the details, but I do remember feeling sick to my stomach as we were riding home because I knew that when I got home, my mother would take my score card and intensely question me about why my scores were low, make me recount all of my mistakes, and tell me that I was very disappointing. I did get home and I was interrogated, and during that interrogation I lied. It wasn't even a good lie. My mother asked me why my beam score was so low, and I told her that I didn't do the front aerial. She asked me why and I told her that Mr. Turner had taken it out of my routine and I didn't know why. This lie provided a small window of relief that lasted only until the next day, when before practice, my mother confronted Mr. Turner and he told her the truth that I had failed to tell. My mother went home and Mr. Turner called me into his office. He yelled at me, loudly. It wasn't a private meeting because the whole team could hear what he said. I still remember his words to this day. He said, "You are a liar and a coward. I have no respect for a liar and a coward. You will change your behavior, or I will kick you off this team. I don't care how good you are, there is no place on this team for a liar and a coward." I faced a similar conversation when I got home after practice.

His words left a lasting imprint on my soul because I deeply believed every word he said. For me, his words were not simply about my inability to overcome my fear of doing a trick on the balance beam. Nor were they about a moment when I took the easy way out and dodged some criticism through a lie. I heard his words as a definition of my character. They informed my internal voice and shaped my understanding of myself. His words became a cloak of shame I would wear for years. I still believed these words defined me when I told this story to a Presbyterian minister named Dr. Weston fifteen years later. It was the first time I had ever told this story because the story was a source of deep shame for me. Dr. Weston looked at me with love and said, "You know, I don't condone lying but what is a little girl to do?" He pointed out that I was young and powerless, and overwhelmed by fear. It wasn't brave or noble to lie. It wasn't even helpful, but it was a way to protect myself for a moment when I could not hear any more, could not take any more belittling.

I don't think my story has much in common with the story of the woman with the hemorrhage except for this. Remembering my story helps me to touch the feelings of

isolation, shame, and desperation the woman with the hemorrhage might have experienced as she made her way through
the crowd. I can appreciate how the overwhelming nature of
her suffering shaped her hope, so that she wasn't looking for
anything except for the bleeding to stop. I can appreciate that
the rules of social convention can be good and may be necessary but often don't work well for a person overwhelmed
by oppression. Most importantly, when I get under the skin
of this woman, I more clearly hear the compassion of Jesus.
I hear it in his actions: stopping amid a crowd, stopping in
the midst of his mission to heal the daughter of an important
official. I hear it in his defiance of the questioning crowd who
wonder how he could possibly know that someone touched
him and think it ridiculous that he has stopped to inquire
about the woman. I hear it in his willingness to listen to the
woman's whole truth. Finally, I hear it in his words as he says,
"Daughter your faith has made you well; go in peace, and be
healed of your disease."

The woman's suffering shaped her hope, whittled it
down to a tiny ember, so that all she wanted was to be free
of her disease and sneak away again to the silence of the margins of life where she had no one and nothing. And yet, this
small ember of hope was enough to bring her to Jesus. Jesus's
compassion would not allow for a limited, impersonal healing. Instead, Jesus met this unnamed, unknown woman in
the place suffering had carved out for her. His humanity met
her humanity in that desolate wilderness outside the rules of
conventional society, and he saw her there, saw the fullness
of her suffering and the fullness of the hope she could not
see or articulate for herself. In that lonely place, Jesus met
her face-to-face and that meeting called her forth from her
limited vision of hope to a transformative encounter with
God's mercy that would stop at nothing short of her full

restoration to health in mind, body, soul, and spirit, the fullness of Shalom. Jesus saw the thin glimmer of light that could not be extinguished, even under the torrent of the pain of her darkness, and met her there so that she might "have life, and have it abundantly" (John 10:10).

CHAPTER 5

Becoming Home

As soon as they left the synagogue, they entered the house of Simon and Andrew, with James and John. Now Simon's mother-in-law was in bed with a fever, and they told him about her at once. He came and took her by the hand and lifted her up. Then the fever left her, and she began to serve them.

Mark 1:29–31

One of my most treasured possessions is a bookmark my daughter Molly made for me when she was in college. Molly was working in a secondhand clothing store in Ligonier, Pennsylvania, the summer between her freshman and sophomore year and was often bored. In order to alleviate her boredom one day, she made me a bookmark, drawn with pen on white paper and then laminated. The bookmark is brimming with life. Around the edges of the bookmark are symbols of vitality: flowers dripping with water, vines, bees, leaves, and hearts. In the center of the bookmark is my name, Dr. Patricia Sharbaugh, and beneath that our house in Ligonier. The house, though recognizable in the drawing, is embellished with the feeling of home. Connecting the house and the letter *g* in Sharbaugh is a plant and written into the leaves and swirling vines of the plant are the names of the members of our family, my husband, John, my son, Patrick, and my daughters, Rebecca and Molly.

Surrounding these central bookmark images are symbols rich with meaning. There is a wooden cross and an open book filled in with the names of the seminary and the colleges from which I earned degrees. There is a tart burner, a hot mug of coffee, and a lit candle, symbols that are associated with the little nook in my home where you can always find me first thing in the morning, reading, writing in my journal, praying, and waking up to my day. There are symbols that speak clearly and specifically to the relationship I have with my daughter Molly. Three book titles are listed: *A Tree Grows in Brooklyn*, *The Secret Life of Bees*, and *Ramona the Pest*. Reading these books to Molly when she was a child provided some of the most intimate and wonderful moments we had together in the years she was part of the air that I breathed. Taylor Swift's name appears on the bookmark along with a few musical notes, symbolizing the love Molly and I share for her music and our joyful memories of attending two of her concerts. Most precious are the lyrics from Taylor Swift's music that find their way onto my bookmark, "I had the best day with you today." These lyrics are taken from a song Swift wrote for her mother, a song of gratitude for the steadfast, constant, freely given love of her mother. Their appearance on my bookmark speaks of Molly's gratitude to me as well. Molly's bookmark gift to me is a treasure pointing to the inexpressible love that is the source of our life together as a family. It captures the stability of our lives in a house that somehow magically, beautifully, and surely by God's grace became a home, rich, full, and vibrantly life giving. Together as a family, we became more than any one of us could possibly be on our own, richer than any individual, becoming a deeply connected community blossoming with life.

Houses are places of deep significance for all of us. The houses in which we live become homes, and whether or not these homes are places of safety, nurture, and growth for us, places of abuse, terror, and loneliness, or ambiguous places of both love and wounding, we have deep emotional connections to home. Homes are private places, places of intimate relationships, and can be places where we let go of public demands and expectations, remove our masks, and live as fully as possible as our authentic selves, places where we share with and care for those we consider our nearest and dearest. When we are invited into the home of a friend, our relationship with that friend deepens. We come to know that friend in a way that we did not know them before.

The healing of Peter's mother-in-law takes place in a house that is the home of Simon (Peter) and Andrew. Jesus leaves a place of public teaching and healing, the synagogue, and with James and John, enters the house of Simon and Andrew. There is an immediate shift from Jesus's public life to a personal private sphere as he is told that someone in the family, Peter's mother-in-law, is sick with a fever. Homes in first-century Capernaum typically housed extended families; we are told that this house was home to at least two brothers, Andrew and Peter, and included Peter's mother-in-law and most likely his wife and perhaps children as well. Most homes during this time would have an entranceway that would open into a central courtyard with multiple rooms surrounding the courtyard.[1] The rooms themselves were often dark, sometimes windowless, and were used primarily for sleeping and for taking shelter in bad weather. Much of the living space was outdoors and the majority of household activity took place out in the open.[2]

When Jesus is told that Peter's mother-in-law is sick

with a fever, he goes to her, enters the private space where she is lying, takes her by the hand, and helps her up. Commentaries on this passage mention that touching is characteristic of Jesus's ministry and that the desire of the suffering to be touched is also common.[3] Perhaps this is an indication of the personal dimension of healing; it is not an impersonal force, but a relationship with Jesus that heals. We are told that Jesus helps her up, literally raises her up, restoring her to health.[4] What we get from the story is a brief glimpse into the private lives of Jesus and his disciples. We get to see them in the intimate setting of a private home, and because of this we see that both in public and private life, Jesus was known as a healer. Jesus brings his healing presence into the intimacy of that home and, through touch, restores Peter's mother-in-law to health. Her response to being healed is to serve, a term rich in meaning that we will explore much more fully momentarily.

This story is so short, so simple that it can be easily over-looked. Yet, a deeper dimension of the story emerges if we pay attention to its placement in the first chapter of Mark's Gospel. The story is part of a collection of stories that characterize the beginning of Jesus's Galilean ministry. These stories paint a picture for us of the typical activities that characterize Jesus's ministry. Jesus calls disciples, teaches, exorcises demons, cures and heals many people, gets up early in the morning to go off by himself to pray, leaves Capernaum to minister to people in other nearby villages, and then returns to Capernaum. When the story of Jesus healing Peter's mother-in-law is read in the context of these other stories, two important aspects of the story emerge. First, this house in Capernaum is central to Jesus's early ministry, and second, the story is not simply about healing, it is also about discipleship.

In the first chapter of Mark's Gospel, Jesus comes to the house in Capernaum and heals Peter's mother-in-law; this house then becomes the location for many more healings. "That evening, at sundown, they brought to him all who were sick or possessed with demons. And the whole city was gathered around the door" (Mark 1:32–33). The spreading recognition of the ministry of Jesus is centered in this house in Capernaum, is evident on its front doorstep. When Jesus gets up very early to pray the next morning, he is told, "Everyone is searching for you" (1:37). When people were looking for Jesus, they were looking for him at the house in Capernaum. Jesus understands that his mission calls him to leave Capernaum and to go out to "neighboring towns," and yet after he goes out to these towns, he returns to Capernaum, a place that is described as his home. "When he returned to Capernaum after some days, it was reported that he was at home" (Mark 2:1). It is unclear whether this home indicates a different house that Jesus now lived in, or whether it was the very house in which Jesus healed Peter's mother-in-law.[5] What is important for us to note is that in the first few chapters of Mark's Gospel, chapters that describe the beginning of Jesus's ministry, this house in Capernaum was a stable and central place for Jesus, a place that Jesus went forth from and a place to which he returned.

Archeologists have identified this house in Capernaum. The house lies between the remains of an ancient synagogue and the Sea of Galilee. The history of the house is told through archeological evidence. The house began as a simple family home and, in the first century, was converted into a public meeting place. The walls were plastered and writing on the walls speaks of Jesus as Christ and Lord, indicating that this house served as an early house church for the Christian community. The archeological evidence is supported by evidence from the diaries and travel journals of fourth- to sixth-century pilgrims who visited the site. The travel diary of Egeria, a fourth-century pilgrim, records this, "In Capernaum a house church was made out of the house of Peter, and its walls still stand today."[6] In the fifth century, an octagonal church was built that enclosed the original structure and marked it as a sacred place. Today there is a church built over the ruins of that fifth-century church. It has a glass floor that allows visitors to look down into the ruins.[7]

The centrality of the house in Capernaum is vital information as we begin to more fully explore what is meant by the last words of our story, "Then the fever left her, and she began to serve them" (Mark 1:31). The Greek word translated here as "serve" can also be translated as "to wait on" or "to minister." It is an important word that appears at key points in Mark's Gospel. When Jesus is in the wilderness after his baptism, this word is used to describe the angels who wait on him (Mark 1:13). The New American Bible translates the word differently, telling us that the angels minister to Jesus and Peter's mother-in-law waits on them (Jesus and his disciples). When Jesus teaches his disciples about the purpose and meaning of discipleship, he uses this word to describe both discipleship and his own mission (Mark 9:35; 10:44–45). The word *deacon* is derived from this Greek word, an office we associate with ministry and service to the church.

Commenting on the story of the healing of Peter's mother-in-law in *The Women's Bible Commentary*, Mary Ann Tolbert writes,

> English versions translate the verb designating her actions as "serve," which is acceptable as long as the same translation has been used for this word in its first appearance in the story in Mark 1:13, but some of those translations render the first occurrence as "the angels *ministered* to him." Translating the same Greek word as "minister" when angels are

the subject but "serve" when a woman is the subject downplays her action.[8]

The concern expressed here is valid and springs from sensitiv-
ity to gender roles and the dearth of leadership positions for
women in the church throughout its two-thousand-year-old
history. I do think translation matters and I also find myself
frustrated when words are translated one way for men, or in
this case angels, and another for women. Despite this frustra-
tion though, I find myself noticing that downplaying the action
of Peter's mother-in-law begins not in the translation but in the
simplicity and terseness of the story. I already mentioned that
the story is easily overlooked and I think that maybe this is
because the action of Peter's mother-in-law, her service to the
church, was the service associated with stability, with everyday
life, with the ordinary, and this service always has been and
probably always will be overlooked even though it is a vital,
life-giving form of discipleship.

In Mark's Gospel, two actions are associated with discipleship, to follow and to serve.[9] In Capernaum, Jesus calls
Simon, Andrew, James, and John to follow him. He then heals
Peter's mother-in-law and she serves. Both activities, following and serving, are forms of discipleship, but our gospel stories focus much more on those that follow. We don't hear as
much about those who serve, the ones who provide the stability behind the scenes, and while we recognize that service
is essential and central to Jesus's own mission, this unseen,
unrecognized service is still as problematic for us today as it
was in the time of Jesus.

I work at St. Vincent College, a school founded by Benedictine monks. The college is located on the property of the
first Benedictine monastery in the United States, a monastery that continues to be the largest in the country. There are
between 150 and 160 monks committed to this monastery.

The monks have a strong presence on campus: there are monks who serve as the college president, as campus minister, as members of the faculty, and even as head of security on campus. Most Benedictine monks wear long black cassocks, and I have become so accustomed to seeing them that sometimes when I am off campus at a restaurant or bookstore and someone enters wearing a black rain coat, my first thought is, "Oh, which monk has come to the bookstore?"

Benedictine monks take three vows when they commit their lives fully to their vocation, the vows of stability, obedience, and *conversatio morum*, which roughly translates "conversion of life." The three vows are deeply related to one another.[10] At the heart of the call to stability is the desire to commit not merely to one place and to find God in that place, but to become the stable place where God dwells and where others can come to find God. This internal stability is related to and formed through outer stability and happens only through deep listening, the real meaning of obedience, and allowing one's heart to soften and change over many years, a lifetime even. Books on monastic spirituality abound with the difficulty and challenge of stability and yet lives of stability do not lend themselves to great literary works. A quick walk through the library stacks is all that is needed to see that literature is heavily weighted toward the topic of journeys. Remaining in one place for life is not a subject that makes for thrilling page turners. One of the few who has been able to capture the adventure of a life of stability is the Trappist Monk Thomas Merton. As I have read about Merton and read Merton, it has occurred to me how very necessary, how life saving, stability was for Merton, how he sometimes chaffed against it, and how deeply rich, creative, and life giving his writing is because of it.

Relationship is at the heart of the monastic vows of stability, obedience, and *conversatio morum*; a relationship with

God lived out in and through the relationships in the community. The monastic community is to be a "school for the Lord's service," a place in which individuals can encounter, learn from, and be changed by God's grace in and through one another. This might be the reason Benedict dedicates the longest chapter in the Rule to humility. Humility is a relational virtue, a virtue that goes unnoticed but, like oxygen for the body, is an essential element of a truly loving community.

In a book about living the Rule of Benedict in today's world, Joan Chittister opens her chapter on humility by describing the significance of the central courtyard for her monastic community. She discusses the flowers that grow there, the spaciousness of the courtyard, the light that the courtyard provides, and how this life-giving oasis that might be described by some as wasted space, captures the heart of monastic life. In today's world, a place dedicated to empty space is as misunderstood as a life dedicated to prayer, to one place, and to service to God. Productivity, demonstrations of power, assertion of individualism through materialism, and loud opinions based on surface assumptions seem to be what is valued; not empty space that allows for growth, beauty, peace, and light. Chittister relates the courtyard she describes to the Rule,

> Yet, the courtyard is one of the most life-giving places we have. It gives light to the inside of the monastery. It breeds beauty. Much like a Japanese garden, it centers the house in peace. And everybody knows it. And few people see it. But without it the house would be a completely different place.
>
> Benedict does that with his chapter on humility. He places it inconspicuously in the center of the Rule, and it leavens the entire document, the entire way of life.[11]

Humble people are like the courtyard Chittister describes. They go unnoticed, unseen, but without them the house, whether a family home or a monastic community, is a completely different place. Humble people are stable, earthed, and their stability welcomes others, allows room for others to grow, and nurtures the roots of life so that purposeful and meaningful journeys can be made.

When describing Molly's bookmark at the beginning of this chapter, I talked about our house as a place of stability, a place where God's grace was encountered by all of us, a place we became most fully ourselves, a place of deep, loving connections, a place blossoming with life. The same daughter who made me that bookmark also wrote this birthday wish on my husband John's Facebook page:

> Happy Birthday to the BEST DAD IN THE WHOLE WORLD John Sharbaugh!!!! I am truly blessed with the best Dad a girl could ever have. My Dad is the nicest, most selfless human on earth. He is my support, strength, and humor. In every novel, TV show, or movie that has a really wonderful Dad character, I always think, "my Dad is a million billion times better." I am so blessed that my Dad was born, and that I have him for a Dad. I love you, Dad. Happy Birthday!!!

After my sister-in-law Eileen read this post, she told me that while there are many messages of this type on Facebook pages, this one rang particularly true. I agree with her. I am convinced that our house became the loving, life-giving home it did because of the stability and humility of my husband, John.

When I think back to the beginning of my relationship with John in the college where we met, I remember two things. I remember that he could always make me laugh, and I remember that getting to know him was like unwrapping a present of priceless value that no one else had the privilege of receiving. Thirty-five years or so have passed since we first met, and I have never had a day without laughter or without a moment when I have felt deeply cared for, deeply loved. John notices me. He notices the things other people don't notice, the person I am beneath the mask I put on to please people. He loves that person and I don't think there is a gift more valuable than being loved for who you really are, except maybe seeing that person love your children in that same beautiful way.

I don't think I can capture John on paper, so two small stories will have to suffice. John and I have a two-year-old granddaughter named Eliza. She is adorable, smart, and beautiful. Every week John comes home with some special treat that he has picked up for Eliza: a puzzle, a book, crayons, stickers. John's way of giving presents is to leave them to be found. He doesn't even have to be there to see the person receive the gift and has no need for them to know that he is the giver. His joy comes from knowing that the gift will bring them joy. But more important than all the gifts he could possibly give to Eliza is his gift for entering her world. We recently took a walk on a rainy day. The walk was initiated because Eliza was tired, a bit cranky, and seemed to need to get out of the house. Now if I had been the sole adult with Eliza, I would have put her in the stroller and walked quietly and peacefully down the street hoping she might fall asleep. This is not John's way. John, who was wearing his slippers, ran with the stroller zigzagging down the street so that he could steer the stroller through all the deepest puddles he could find. His feet got soaked, the stroller was drenched, and Eliza was delighted. It is an unreasonable way to walk with a child if you are hoping for calm and order, but if you want to feed the child's sense of adventure, to help them fall in love with the world, there is no better method.

The second story I will tell is this. When our daughter Rebecca was getting ready to start college at Notre Dame, she received her class schedule in the mail. She was about to move seven hours away from home, something none of us could quite imagine. One Saturday, John sat with Rebecca on the couch in our living room and, using her computer and the maps on Notre Dame's website, walked with her through her entire schedule. He showed her the best route to every class, talked about where she could eat, where she would buy books, how to find the ATM. It wasn't just that he showed her where to go, it was more that he joined her in that experience, so patiently, so calmly giving her the message that even though she would be away from home, home would be with her, would accompany her, would give her the strength necessary to embark on this very big and important journey.

These stories merely brush the surface of how John's humility and stability shaped our family. His quiet, faithful way of waiting on us may have been invisible to everyone else in the world, but none of us would be where we are, or be who we are without it. It is this service that centered our family in peace, this stability that made possible the spaciousness necessary for becoming, for laughing, for loving. It is this service that allowed the rest of us to go out into the world and risk adventure.

When Jesus leaves a public place of holiness, the synagogue, and enters into the home of Peter's mother-in-law, that home becomes a place of holiness, a place where God's grace is encountered, a place that heals. It isn't the place that is important but the relationships within that place that make it holy. This private house in Capernaum becomes a source of stability for Jesus's Galilean ministry and later becomes a public worship space, but the real source of holiness in that place came from a relationship with Jesus that led to discipleship in the form of service. A humble, behind-the-scenes service, unnoticed, perhaps downplayed, not followed by the gospel writers who concentrate on the more interesting stories of those who journey with Jesus, but this form of discipleship was essential for the early church and continues to change lives, and to be formative and life giving to countless families and countless communities. The story of Peter's mother-in-law is the story of all the people who encounter God and then commit to tireless, unselfish, patient service in one place, becoming for others the home where they might find both God and themselves. "God is love, and those who abide in love abide in God, and God abides in them" (1 John 4:16).

CHAPTER 6

As Darkness Approaches

From there he set out and went away to the region of
Tyre. He entered a house and did not want anyone to
know he was there. Yet he could not escape notice,
but a woman whose little daughter had an unclean
spirit immediately heard about him, and she came
and bowed down at his feet. Now the woman was a
Gentile, of Syrophoenician origin. She begged him to
cast the demon out of her daughter. He said to her,
"Let the children be fed first, for it is not fair to take
the children's food and throw it to the dogs." But she
answered him, "Sir, even the dogs under the table eat
the children's crumbs." Then he said to her, "For saying
that, you may go—the demon has left your daughter."
So she went home, found the child lying on the bed,
and the demon gone.

Mark 7:24–30

I harbor a secret desire. The desire is born from observing that
when I read a book or watch a movie for a second time,
I notice so many more details, small connections between

scenes, so many nuances that escaped my notice the first time through when concern with the plot, with how the story was going to turn out occupied my thoughts. My desire is to apply this second time book-reading, movie-watching observation to my life. Now that my children are grown up and have successfully moved into their own lives, I wish I could live it all over again. Read their lives for a second time. Relive their births and all the events and everyday moments of their childhood days knowing ahead of time how it all turns out. Imagine what I might notice now that I can relax and really observe what is happening. Of course, this type of desire is only fulfilled in books and movies that involve time travel, and the plots of time travel stories are inevitably complicated by the time-traveling person interfering to help someone and through that intervention causing events to unfold differently. I don't want to change anything, I simply want to see and notice all the wonderful little details I missed the first time through. I want to see it through the lens of certainty that comes from knowing how it all turns out. Unfortunately, life only happens in one direction and while it is happening, we don't know how things are going to turn out. Our anxiety, uncertainty, and recognition of our responsibility to do what is right in each moment so that the future will turn out the way we hope and pray that it will, prevents us from seeing clearly and completely.

This is a pertinent observation as we turn to our gospel story. The encounter between Jesus and the Syrophoenician woman intrigues and perplexes us. We can easily relate to some aspects of the story. While we don't ordinarily see Jesus moving into less familiar territory in order to be alone, I think we can all relate to his desire for a time away in order to rest and to recover enthusiasm and energy for the task at hand. The mother with a sick child desperately seeking out, willingly crossing boundaries, and boldly interrupting a healer's time away is also an aspect of the story that is easily grasped. Jesus's uncharacteristic response to her respectful plea for help, however, is quite unexpected as is his change of heart in response to her comeback. The woman's unwavering persistence in the face of Jesus's insulting denial and her creative turn of phrase surprises us. When we read this encounter, we can feel the tension underlying the meeting between Jesus and this woman. In this biblical story, we are confronted with the humanity of Jesus and we walk away with questions. Why doesn't Jesus simply heal her daughter when she first falls at his feet and makes her request? Why does he compare her to a dog? Why does he change his mind? Does he change his mind? Is it really possible that Jesus learns something from this foreign woman about his own mission? These questions are all troubling because they challenge us at the root of our faith, our understanding of Jesus as the Christ. If Jesus is the Son of God, surely he knows that his mission of salvation is for all people, not only the children of Israel. Surely, he is certain of the abundance of God's mercy.

This story perplexes us because we are reading it backward, from the certainty of the future, from and through layers and layers of Christian tradition that have reflected on our certainty of salvation through Jesus Christ. We read that certainty back into the account and find that Jesus's response to the woman doesn't make sense because we think Jesus should be certain about how salvation will unfold. Yet the very human encounter at the heart of this story brings us face-to-face with the reality of Jesus's incarnation in a particular place, in a particular time, as a human being in the midst of an unfolding history. Therefore, in order to begin to understand the story, it is essential to investigate the geographic location of the meeting, its placement in the gospel, and the cultural and societal background of both Jesus and the woman.

Jesus and the Syrophoenician woman meet in a region north of Galilee, in Gentile territory. Referring to the region as Tyre suggests that Jesus is in the lands bordering Galilee and under the jurisdiction of Tyre. In the prophetic literature of the Old Testament, Tyre is associated with spreading terror throughout the world and arrogantly amassing wealth (Ezek 26:17; Zech 9:3).[1] The Jewish historian Josephus describes the inhabitants of Tyre as bitter enemies of the Jews, who killed and imprisoned many Jews in the Jewish War of AD 66. During the time of Jesus, rural Galilee served as the breadbasket for Tyre, supplying food to its wealthier inhabitants while many Galileans went hungry.[2] The significance of identifying the region Jesus enters as Tyre is to indicate that Jesus has not only entered Gentile territory, but territory that is associated with hostility toward the Jewish people.[3] Identifying the Syrophoenician woman as Greek and indicating that her daughter lies on a bed rather than a mattress alert the reader that this mother likely comes from the social class of Tyre that is oppressing the Jewish people. This is important to remember because we tend to think of Jesus as the more powerful partner in this conversation when this wealthy Greek woman may have been more powerful in the culture than Jesus was.[4]

Jesus comes to this place of potential hostility after rising up to leave a place where he has encountered conflict with the Pharisees and the scribes. The Pharisees and scribes accuse Jesus of not following the oral traditions of the fathers concerning purity and washing rituals for eating. Jesus confronts the Pharisees and scribes and returns home, only to find that even his own disciples have not understood his teaching. The importance of these small controversies and misunderstandings is magnified when attention is paid to the placement of these stories in the context of Mark's Gospel.

Most interpreters of Mark's Gospel recognize that the

Gospel unfolds in two parts.[5] In chapters 1—8, Jesus is in charge, active, and successful. He announces the coming of God's kingdom and initiates that coming through his actions in every place he goes. Jesus teaches with authority, heals, exorcises demons, gathers and leads disciples. Wherever Jesus goes, people recognize him and follow him. This part of the Gospel takes place mainly in Galilee, and while there are a few controversies along the way, if we painted this first half of Mark's Gospel, it would be bright. The painting would radiate light, optimism, the feeling that God's way in the world makes sense. Beginning in chapter 8, however, things begin to change. Jesus begins to talk about his suffering and death; the disciples don't understand what he is trying to tell them. Increasingly, controversy surrounds him, and after his arrest, he is no longer the one who is acting but the one who is acted upon: arrested, beaten, put to death on a cross. The painting from the second half of the Gospel would definitely take on darker hues and express feelings of disquiet, a sense of foreboding, confusion, and sadness. The story about Jesus's encounter with the Syrophoenician woman lies right at the heart of the transition from the first half of the Gospel into the second and has something to say to us about boundary crossing, about discernment, about faith, and about giving your life to God.

Theologian Jon Sobrino points out that the transition from light to darkness in Mark's Gospel is not merely external but is an expression of a transition within Jesus himself. Writing about Jesus's faith as an essential element of Jesus's humanity, Sobrino discusses the historical unfolding of that faith.[6] He claims that it isn't that Jesus's understanding of God or his mission changes, since he begins his mission with complete trust and total commitment to God his father and complete and total commitment to his mission of ushering in the kingdom of God, and he dies on the cross with complete trust and total commitment to God his father and for the sake of bringing God's kingdom to bear on the world. But even though Jesus's commitment to both God and his mission are complete and unchanging, his experience of his relationship with God and to his mission does change over the course of his three-year ministry. Like all human beings called by God, Jesus begins his mission with optimism and a profound sense of the power of God's presence shaping his life and ministry, but as he continually comes up against evil and injustice, human sin, and human misunderstanding, he is increasingly surrounded by the darkness sin creates. Even though he is without sin, he enters the places where sin reigns and because of this, his relationship with God is increasingly colored by darkness and mystery. Jesus must trust God in the midst of the profound darkness he experiences. The one who proclaims, "Your faith has made you well" (Mark 5:34; 10:52), is led to a place where he, himself, will cry, "My God, my God, why have you forsaken me?" (Mark 15:34).

I think Sobrino's articulation of the historical unfolding of Jesus's faith is helpful when reading the story of the encounter between Jesus and the Syrophoenician woman. We are inclined to think only of obvious moments in Jesus's life when the darkness surrounded him. We think of his time in the desert of temptation, or in the garden of Gethsemane, or on the cross, but dying to self, giving oneself completely to God and to the work God has called us to do doesn't happen in isolated instances; it is a process, a practice lived out day by day, moment by moment.

I recently went to the beach with my family, and while I was there, I read a novel. Through the main character in the novel, the writer expressed his opinion that in the course of a lifetime there are only a few moments, key moments, that really matter, and most of our lives, the time in between these moments, is wasted. I completely disagree with this author's view of life. I think every moment of life matters and the more we open our hearts to God, the more each moment is a moment, or has the potential to be a moment, in which we encounter God, through nature, through our daily activities, and through the people we meet along the way. Jesus's encounter with the Syrophoenician woman is a window through which we can see Jesus living out his human faith and trust in God in his day-to-day life.

The meeting between Jesus and the Syrophoenician woman, like many of our own encounters with people, occurs at a time that is difficult for both of them. The opening of this story specifically tells us that Jesus went into the district of Tyre and entered a house in order to escape notice. He desired to be away from others and instead is encountered by this distraught mother. Anyone who is a mother can easily relate to the woman's situation. She is fighting for her daughter. This is not the time for polite conversation. There is a sense of urgency for both Jesus and the woman. The misunderstandings and controversies that Jesus has recently experienced have awakened within him the sense that he is moving toward a time when darkness and misunderstanding will increasingly color his path. The woman is seeking healing for her daughter and will stop at nothing, is willing to risk anything and everything in order to draw attention to her daughter's plight. Though they have just met, their encounter begins in a deep place. Their respective situations have already stripped them of self-consciousness and pretense, and they dive right into the heart of the matter.

The beating heart of the matter is the abundance of God's mercy. This may not be apparent at first because the dialogue between Jesus and the Syrophoenician woman gets off to a rough start. This distraught mother, who symbolizes people who have been oppressing the Jewish people for centuries, begs Jesus, a Jew, to cast an unclean spirit from her daughter. Jesus surprises us by drawing attention to boundaries. He says, "Let the children be fed first, for it is not fair to take the children's food and throw it to the dogs." This statement indicates that Jesus understood his mission to be to Israel and this woman is a Gentile, a group the Jews sometimes referred to as dogs.[7] This comment seems so uncharacteristic of Jesus that it catches everyone off guard. Interpreters try to get around this statement by saying things like Jesus was only testing the woman or by pointing out that the Greek word used for *dog* is a diminutive meaning "puppy." One commentator even writes, "We can be quite sure that the smile on Jesus' face and the compassion in his eyes robbed the words of all insult and bitterness."[8] I don't think we can get around Jesus's comment so easily. We must take it seriously and ask for a moment why he might say this.

Jesus's identity is tied to his mission; his understanding of himself and his understanding of his mission are thoroughly Jewish. We read the Gospels and we remember Jesus's conflicts with some Pharisees, scribes, and Sadducees: conflicts over ritual purity, healing on the Sabbath, meal sharing, and resurrection.[9] These conflicts are about practices that were commonly disputed in first-century Palestine, however and therefore, even Jesus's opposition to these Jewish teachers and leaders is part of his participation in Jewish practice. We tend to remember these conflicts without reflecting on how everything Jesus says and does is rooted in Judaism: his understanding of God, his teaching, his healing ministry, all of it was learned in and springs from Judaism.

Though thoroughly Jewish, Jesus does not refrain from challenging his Jewish brothers and sisters. Furthermore, Jesus has already healed in Gentile territory. He healed the Geresene demoniac, sending the unclean spirits into a herd of pigs (Mark 5:1–20). Jesus is not opposed to healing Gentiles in need or to challenging Jewish practice. So why does he hesitate to heal the Syrophoenician's daughter? The issue must lie, I think, in the identification of the woman with people openly and actively opposed to Judaism. Jesus's identity is rooted in his Jewish practice, and he understands his mission as a mission to the Jewish people, and now in this foreign place, he is being challenged to show God's mercy to people who have a history of actively seeking to oppress God's people. Jesus's words in Mark's Gospel indicate that Jesus understands that God's mercy will go out to others after it fills the children of Israel, but he does not think that time has come yet. That is why the Syrophoenician woman's response to Jesus is so powerful.

The Syrophoenician does not challenge Jesus's understanding of his mission, she supports it. She calls him Lord, an indication that she understands who he is.[10] She agrees that his mission is to the children of Israel, but she simply points to the abundance of God's mercy. God's mercy is so abundant that others, Gentiles and, yes, even enemies of Israel do not have to wait for the children to be fed. The crumbs of God's mercy that fall beneath the table are more than enough. In pointing to the abundance of God's saving mercy, this woman joins the best practitioners of petitionary prayer in Jewish history who for the sake of others ask God to show mercy, practitioners like Abraham (Gen 18), Moses (Exod 32), and all the unnamed lamenters of the Psalms. Jesus hears what this woman says and tells her that because of her word, her daughter has been healed. The woman reminds Jesus, the revelation of God's mercy in the world, of the abundance of that mercy, and Jesus, who is facing darkness, is open enough to hear what she says and to respond. These two people meet in their encounter with darkness and find in one another a bounty of light.

As I have been researching, praying, and thinking about this encounter amid darkness, I have been reminded of another man, Dietrich Bonhoeffer, who in the face of approaching darkness left a record of profound encounters. Bonhoeffer, born in Germany in 1906, was a minister and theologian who is remembered most for the way that he lived his Christian faith. Bonhoeffer's faith was lived out day to day, moment by moment, as he listened for and discerned the way God was calling him to resist Hitler and the Nazis, and to share in the sufferings of the German people during Hitler's reign. The path Bonhoeffer walked led to his imprisonment in Tegel prison and eventually his death in Flossenbürg on April 9, 1945.

A collection of Bonhoeffer's writings during his two-year imprisonment, *Letters and Papers from Prison*, reveals the depth of Bonhoeffer's faith and how this faith shaped his encounters with others. The collection is a stunning record of the power of faith to transform a potentially isolating experience into a time of profound encounter. Though in prison and unable to attend important family events such as baptisms and marriages, Bonhoeffer participates in and is profoundly present at these events through his letters. Bonhoeffer also formed bonds of friendship with his fellow prisoners, sharing in conversation with them, offering them hope, and giving them strength. These relationships crossed many boundaries. One of his dialogue partners in prison was an atheist, and when Bonhoeffer was asked to lead a worship service, he hesitated out of concern that this friend might feel excluded. Bonhoeffer's strength to be present to these encounters even as the darkness overtook his own life lay in the hope he found through faith. The day before he died, Bonhoeffer led a worship service in a schoolroom that had become a makeshift prison cell for Bonhoeffer and his fellow prisoners as they journeyed toward Flossenbürg, where he would be hung. During this service, his fellow prisoner S. Payne Best remembers that Bonhoeffer "spoke to us in a manner which reached the hearts of all, finding just the right words to express the spirit of our imprisonment and the thoughts and resolutions which it had brought."[11] When some men came for Bonhoeffer to escort him to his final destination, Bonhoeffer said to Best, "This is the end, for me the beginning of life."[12] Bonhoeffer's hope came from knowing that in and through his death he was handing himself over to God. Yet even more importantly, knowing that he would hand himself over to God in his death shaped everything he did in his life, shaped his choices, and was the beating heart in all his encounters. Walking this way, practicing faith, living from trust in the face of darkness was not without cost, however. That cost is apparent in a poem Bonhoeffer wrote while in prison called "Who Am I?"

Who Am I?

Who am I? They often tell me
I would step from my cell's confinement
calmly, cheerfully, firmly,
like a squire from his country-house.

Who am I? They often tell me
I would talk to my warders
freely and friendly and clearly,
as though it were mine to command.

Who am I? They also tell me
I would bear the days of misfortune
equably, smilingly, proudly,
like one accustomed to win.

Am I then really all that which other men tell of?
Or am I only what I know of myself,
restless and longing and sick, like a bird in a cage,

struggling for breath, as though hands were
    compressing my throat,
yearning for colours, for flowers, for the voices of
    birds,
thirsting for words of kindness, for
    neighbourliness,
trembling with anger at despotisms and petty
    humiliations,
powerlessly trembling for friends at an infinite
    distance,
weary and empty at praying, at thinking, at
    making,
faint, and ready to say farewell to it all?

Who am I? This or the other?
Am I one person today, and tomorrow another?
Am I both at once? A hypocrite before others,
and before myself a contemptibly woebegone
    weakling?
Or is something within me still like a beaten
    army,
fleeing in disorder from victory already achieved?

Who am I? They mock me, these lonely questions
    of mine.
Whoever I am, though knowest, O God, I am
    thine.[13]

The strength Bonhoeffer drew from his faith led him to live a courageous life with and for others, but as the poem shows, sensing the end does not remove the cost and suffering in the moments of the unfolding history of his faith. Moreover, his suffering is not neatly preserved for the last moments of his life but is woven into each moment and decision that leads to that last moment. The story of Jesus's encounter with the Syrophoenician woman is located in Mark's Gospel as Jesus is transitioning from bright, successful days of ministry into days colored by misunderstanding, conflict, suffering, and then death. In the midst of that transition, Jesus encounters this distraught mother who is suffering in her own darkness. This very human encounter between Jesus and this mother allows us to glimpse the moment-to-moment cost and suffering that were part of Jesus's ministry of God's abundant mercy. Jesus, our elder brother in faith (Heb 2:17), shows us that even though we faithfully look forward to the resurrection from the dead, even when we live knowing that in the end, we will hand our lives over to God, we still feel the weight of responsibility, experience uncertainty about how to respond to enemies, feel the cost and the suffering of living out our trust in God's abundant mercy as darkness approaches.

A sermon I heard years ago on the cost of living out our faith moment to moment has stayed with me.[14] In this sermon, Fred Craddock relates that when he first became a Christian, he often thought about martyrdom. He would hear Jesus ask him, "Fred, can you drink the cup that I drink?" (see Mark 10:39). Craddock says that he thought he could. But when he pictured this martyrdom, it was always sudden and dramatic. He would picture himself standing before a firing squad and asked, "Do you believe in Jesus Christ?" He would answer yes and die in a blaze of gunfire. After years of practicing Christianity, Craddock claims he has come to understand that martyrdom does not often look the way he imagined it would. Instead, he now understands that most Christians are asked to drink from the same cup as Jesus, one sip at a time, every day, for the rest of their lives.

CHAPTER 7

Hidden in Christ

Now as they went on their way, he entered a certain village, where a woman named Martha welcomed him into her home. She had a sister named Mary, who sat at the Lord's feet and listened to what he was saying. But Martha was distracted by her many tasks; so she came to him and asked, "Lord, do you not care that my sister has left me to do all the work by myself? Tell her then to help me." But the Lord answered her, "Martha, Martha, you are worried and distracted by many things; there is need of only one thing. Mary has chosen the better part, which will not be taken away from her."

Luke 10:38–42

Pedro Arrupe, a Spanish Jesuit priest who served as the twenty-eighth Superior General of the Society of Jesus, tells a story about experiencing hospitality in a desperately poor slum in Latin America. Fr. Arrupe was visiting some Jesuit priests who were living and serving in the region when, after saying Mass, he encountered a local man who invited him to his home. He recounts this story in a book of interviews called *One Jesuit's Spiritual Journey*:

> When it was over, a big devil whose hang-dog look made me almost afraid said, "Come to my place. I have something to give you." I was undecided; I didn't know whether to accept or not, but the priest who was with me said, "Accept, Father, they are good people." I went to his place; his house was a hovel nearly on the point of collapsing. He had me sit down on a rickety old chair. From there I could see the sunset. The big man said to me, "Look, sir, how beautiful it is!" We sat in silence for several minutes. The sun disappeared. The man then said, "I don't know how to thank you for all you have done for us. I have nothing to give you, but I thought you would like to see this sunset. You liked it didn't you? Good evening." And then he shook my hand.[1]

This story offers us a profound lesson in hospitality. Offering hospitality is paradoxical because while we often associate our hospitality with things, with the material comforts we offer our guests such as good food, a soft bed to sleep in, a warm and inviting atmosphere, these material comforts are really only the surface enhancements of hospitality. The vital component of hospitality is spaciousness, emptiness, providing space that welcomes the mystery of the other. The man who offered hospitality to Fr. Arrupe was familiar with emptiness. Dire poverty had been his teacher and despite the harshness of his forced simplicity, his heart had listened closely in the emptiness and welcomed the hidden fullness of the mystery of the other revealed in the beauty of a sunset. The beauty of light bent to reveal its colors had so generously filled his emptiness that he was compelled to share that fullness with Fr. Arrupe, to offer it as gift. If he had listened to the world, he would think that he had nothing to offer anyone, let alone an important priest and visitor to the region, but because instead he had listened to God, he was confident that his gift was valuable and would be well received. He knew that ultimately he wasn't the real host, God was, and he was just offering another fellow traveler an empty space to share the glimpse of God he had received.

Hospitality is a theme in the story of Martha and Mary, and like many biblical stories with this theme, it is not simple or straightforward.[2] Biblical stories of hospitality often contain an element of mystery. Unexpected guests arrive, unexpected requests are asked in unexpected conditions, unexpected behavior results in unexpected praise, and abundance flows amid scarcity.[3] The story of Martha and Mary contains some of these unexpected elements, and like other biblical stories of hospitality, this story evokes a strong emotional response from its readers.[4]

I teach a course at St. Vincent College called Women in the New Testament, and whenever the class begins to read about Martha and Mary in Luke chapter 10 and in John chapters 11—12, someone in the class will inevitably discuss the fact that as an older sister, they can easily relate to Martha, or as a younger sister they can easily relate to Mary. Moreover, I have had many women in my classes or among my friends tell me that they have been angered by sermons on this passage in Luke. Many women, including myself, have experienced the burden and isolation of cooking for or providing hospitality to many guests, while other members of the family fail to help. No matter how well intentioned, if a sermon focuses on the "fussiness" of Martha in the kitchen while praising the centered calmness of Mary sitting at Jesus's feet in the living room, it leaves a bitter taste in the mouths of all these women who have spent a lot of time and energy in their lives paying attention to all the details that enhance the beauty of life, details that provide wonderful spacious opportunities for communities to form around dinner tables, and in small gatherings of warm friendship. People, women in particular, see themselves in these two sisters, and that makes this particular story both compelling and puzzling.[5]

There are several flaws that have plagued interpretations of the story of Martha and Mary and contributed to misunderstandings about the meaning of the story.[6] One problem is that the story has been read as though it focuses on both sisters equally, pits them against each other, and then chooses Mary as the better model of discipleship. The clear focus of the story, however, is Martha. Martha is the owner of the house, the one who welcomes Jesus, the one who speaks, and the one to whom Jesus addresses his words. Mary is in the background, she is introduced as the sister of Martha, she sits at Jesus's feet, and she listens. If we keep our focus on Martha, we hear the story a bit differently.[7]

A second problem that plagues interpretations of this story follows from the first. At times interpreters of this story have seen in the sisters types of Christian life. Martha represents an active life of discipleship, while Mary represents a contemplative life of discipleship. This form of interpretation takes a story focused on one moment in time and extends it to be the foundation of the whole of life; so while Martha actively serves in this encounter with Jesus, she actively serves every moment of the rest of her life. Likewise, apparently Mary never stands up but spends her entire life at the feet of Jesus![8]

Finally, interpretations of this passage are also complicated by stereotypical images associated with women. Martha's service is often interpreted as cooking and cleaning, even though there is evidence that both Martha and Mary were important leaders in the early Christian movement. The opening of this story in Luke indicates that Martha owned the house to which Jesus and his disciples came. In John's Gospel, Lazarus is identified as the brother of Martha and Mary, an identification that indicates that Martha and Mary were important leaders in the early Christian movement. In this story, Jesus is with his disciples when they stop at the house. Martha's "serving" most likely had to do with a form of ministry that may have included table service but was not necessarily limited to this service.[9]

So let's take a step back. If we keep our focus on Martha, if we recognize that the story is not about pitting either sister or forms of Christian discipleship against one another, we begin to see that the story is meant to teach us a lesson about how to receive Jesus, how to welcome him into our lives. If we listen, the story has a lot to teach us about true hospitality, not about cooking and cleaning, but about finding an interior space that welcomes Christ and in the act of welcoming discovers that Christ has been our host all along.

Invitations to welcome mystery come to us in many forms. Most of us catch a glimpse of mystery from time to time through our encounters with other people, with art, through music, as we watch or participate in sports, as we walk through nature, or hold a baby. There are so many invitations to open our hearts to mystery, and each one of us has certain ways, certain paths that speak to us more clearly than others. For me, one primary way of encountering mystery has been through reading, through books. Stories have always been faithful companions in my life. They have taught me to see the world in new ways and challenged me to open my mind and heart to the stranger.

As a lover of books, I am also quite fond of libraries. The library at St. Vincent College, where I work, has always felt like a welcoming home to me. The main entrance to the library is on the third floor, and in order to access the library

stacks, you descend a spiral staircase. The collection of theological books is on the bottom floor of the library, several
staircases down. Ironically, the room that contains many vol-
umes of theological writing was once the Seminary chapel,
and so this room has always in one way or another welcomed
mystery. For some reason the walk from my office through
hallways, into the main library entrance, and then down
many stairs to the yellow stacks of theology books quiets my
soul and opens my heart to the mystery of my work and the
journey of my life that has brought me to this place. I am
filled with anticipation of the new thoughts about God and
the life of faith that I might find in the books I will check out.
I am filled with the wonder of entering conversations that
have been going on for thousands of years before me. As I
was researching and thinking about the story of Martha and
Mary, I bumbled my way into a very interesting conversation
about hospitality.

My stumbling into this conversation began with some
straightforward research. After I read several commentaries and
articles on Martha and Mary, I decided to do some research
on hospitality in the Rule of Benedict. I thought this research
might help me think through the spiritual practice of hospitality. I began with an article by Benedictine monk and
writer Terrance Kardong, in which he explores the meaning
of chapter 53 of the Rule, a chapter that opens with this: "All
guests who present themselves are to be welcomed as Christ,
for he himself will say: 'I was a stranger and you welcomed
me'" (Matt 25:35).[10] As Kardong explores the meaning of
this chapter, he writes,

> The monastery is like the Church itself in that
> we only remain through the hospitable generos-
> ity of the divine host. We never become "property
> owners" in God's house, entrusted with the duty

of warding off intruders. Our role is to humbly receive the stranger in the same way the Lord has received us....Here is an example of Benedict's incarnational mysticism: in any human interaction, God is encountering God.[11]

I found this thought so compelling that I wanted to explore it more deeply. In a footnote, Kardong tells the reader that he writes more about this concept in another article, and so I set off to find this article.

Finding this article proved to be the first stumble in my otherwise straightforward research efforts. I could not find the article or the journal that Kardong cites, but my efforts to find it led me to journey into the world of the stacks and to page my way through journals. It was then that I ran across a wonderful article on Benedictine hospitality by Demetrius Dumm, OSB, a monk who lived and worked as a teacher, writer, and spiritual leader at St. Vincent Seminary for fifty-seven years before his death in 2013. I was delighted; I had read books and articles by Fr. Dumm before and knew of the quality and spiritual depth of his writing. The article I found by Dumm looks at Benedictine hospitality through the lens of biblical hospitality, and this article gave me the keys I needed to open my heart to receive what the story of Martha and Mary was saying to me.

A short time after I found this article, I ran into Fr. Campion Gavaler, OSB, in the hallway. Fr. Campion was a very close friend of Fr. Dumm. I mentioned the article to him, and even though the article was written over thirty years ago, and even though Fr. Campion is approaching eighty-eight years old, he recalled immediately the heart of the article's message. I told Fr. Campion how I had set out to find one article and had discovered another that fed my imagination and helped me think in new ways. Fr. Campion said, "Isn't that exactly the way life works? You set off in search of one thing, but along the way you find something else that turns out to be exactly what you need."

What I discovered through my walk down a winding, twisted research path is that biblical hospitality involves welcoming the stranger only to discover that in making room for the stranger, we welcome God.[12] The paradigmatic story about hospitality in the Old Testament is the story of Abraham welcoming three strangers at the entrance of his tent near the oaks of Mamre (Gen 18:1–15). Dumm points out that what is most surprising about this story is the exuberance with which Abraham welcomes them. Abraham's enthusiasm is surprising because it is in stark contrast to the disappointment he has been living through. Abraham and Sarah have staked their lives on extravagant promises from God. They left all that they knew to journey to a land God promised in hopes of living there with the descendants God promised them. They believed God's promise of a descendant despite the reality of their advanced ages, and yet, the promised child has not arrived. Abraham's hospitality toward the three strangers who approach his tent reveals his deep faith. Despite heartache and disappointment, Abraham trusts in the ultimate goodness of reality flowing from the goodness of God, and that trust flows into the generous hospitality he offers these men. It turns out that the three strangers represent God, and in welcoming them, Abraham receives the gift he has been waiting and longing for: the strangers tell him that the child of God's promise will be born within the year. Dumm writes,

> It is clear then that the hospitality that Abraham offered to the three strangers was not just an act of pity. Rather, it was a manifestation of his radical faith in God. For God himself had turned mysterious and had become a stranger to Abraham. Yet he persisted

in looking for good in the God whose goodness was once so evident; he looked for a friend in the stranger; he looked for life amid signs of death. Thus, because he was willing to make room for strangers, he also made room for God's surprising gift.[13]

Dumm's article provides several other examples of biblical hospitality, and the common thread that runs through these examples is that in every journey of faith, even the most profound, mystery makes God a stranger and it is through faith lived out in hospitality toward the stranger that one is ushered into the mystery of the presence of God. We are all like the disciples on the road to Emmaus who are walking with Jesus but struggle to recognize him (Luke 24).[14] We struggle because we can never come to understand God; we can only find God by entering a relationship with mystery, by welcoming the stranger. This relationship is both comfort and challenge. It is both familiar and strange. It is both home and wilderness. It is a relationship that is entered into and deepened through trust.

If we listen closely to the story of Martha welcoming Jesus into her home, if we keep our focus on Martha, if we hear what Jesus says to Martha about discipleship, we might hear that Martha's difficulty lies in her lack of trust. She cannot fully welcome the mystery of God's presence in Jesus because she is "worried and distracted by many things" (Luke 10:41). Her anxiety is a symptom of her lack of trust. This is a message we should all be able to relate to because we live in a society characterized by multitasking, distraction, anxiety, and the burden of excessively busy lives. Furthermore, our anxious, multitasking, distraction-filled, excessively busy lives are symptoms of our lack of trust in the goodness of God. Instead of receiving the beautiful gifts of grace available to us throughout the moments of our days, we fill our moments with tasks, agendas, opinions, and activities designed to give us control and make us feel needed. Jesus has shown us the path to walk to find God. It is a path of emptiness, of letting go, of listening deeply for the life God has given us (see Phil 2:6–7).[15] Yet rather than follow the path Jesus has shown us, we grasp, we cling, we fill the silence so we can't hear the voice of God calling, the voice of our neighbors, or even the voice of our own thirsting souls. We can't welcome the mystery of the other because we haven't even begun to receive the mystery of our own lives.

I have a distinct memory of reading about a moment in a young girl's life when I myself was a young girl. I don't remember the name of the book I was reading or the story that surrounded the moment. I do remember that the girl was around fifteen years old, lived several hundred years ago, and the moment in the book I remember is the first time she ever noticed her own face. She leaned over a lake to take a drink of water from her cupped hands and saw her reflection in the lake. The reason I remember reading about this moment is that it was so foreign to my experience. Growing up in a world of photographs, mirrors, and the incessant clamoring of commercials meant to raise anxiety about appearance for the sake of sales, I could not imagine reaching the age of fifteen and not being aware of what I looked like. I have thought about this young girl's experience many times since then. I wonder about how our lives might be shaped differently if we spent our childhood days never noticing the way we looked. If we learned to live first on the inside before we ever paid any attention to the way we looked from the outside. I have longed for the freedom this might bring.

The journey of faith God called me to take was a journey from living a life shaped by others, shaped by what they thought, believed, and wanted from me, to living from an identity I received from God. For me, this journey was as difficult as the journey Israel took through the wilderness. It had great moments of hunger, thirst, regret, discovery, joy, fear, and failure. I had to endure the disappointment of others, hear the clamoring voice of others complaining about me as Martha complained about Mary, "Lord, do you not care that my sister has left me to do all the work by myself? Tell her then to help me" (Luke 10:40). But if I had continued to listen for my life by listening to others, I would not live the life I was called to live.

Thomas Merton writes extensively about the spiritual task of discovering our true identity. Our true selves are "hidden with Christ in God" (Col 3:3). The movement to discover our true self and the movement to discover God is a single movement. In seeking God, we discover the gift of our lives, and in living out the gift of our lives, we discover God. Merton points out the way we play with masks, wearing first one and then another, but that ultimately this wearing of masks to please others and ourselves will not lead us to who we are called to be and therefore to truth and authenticity. Merton writes,

> To work out our own identity in God, which the Bible calls "working out our salvation," is a labor that requires sacrifice and anguish, risk and many tears. It demands close attention to reality at every moment, and great fidelity to God as He reveals Himself, obscurely, in the mystery of each new situation. We do not know clearly beforehand what the result of this work will be. The secret of my full identity is hidden in Him. He alone can make me who I am, or rather who I will be when at last I fully begin to be. But unless I desire this identity and work to find it with Him and in Him, the work will never be done. The way of doing it is a secret I can learn from no one else but Him.[16]

We find our way to ourselves and to God by letting go of our anxiety and worries, and sitting at the feet of Jesus. I don't think this means we are all called to a life of contemplation. Nor do I think this means that we should denigrate the importance of doing good deeds and paying attention to the details of making a welcoming space for others. I do think, though, that if our lives are plagued by anxiety, if we find ourselves habitually distracted and feeling burdened, these are symptoms and perhaps signals that we need to slow down and listen a bit more closely for the life we can only find by drawing close to Christ. Slowing down and listening a bit more closely often involves saying no to things that are good simply because they are not our task to carry out. We have to be willing to risk quiet, to risk loneliness, to risk silence, to risk losing control, to risk being unimportant, to risk hearing others criticizing us for moving at a slower and quieter pace. We need to live in trust in the ultimate goodness of reality flowing from the ultimate goodness of God.

The spiritual life, like all good hospitality, takes time. It is not a life that is nurtured by the fast-paced world of multitasking, distraction, and busyness. It is a life lived by allowing space for silence, for prayer. It is lived by letting go of our constant analysis, letting go of our rational arguments, and simply trusting. Merton writes, "Just go for walks, live in peace, let change come quietly and invisibly on the inside."[17] If we can allow enough space within ourselves to welcome the stranger, we might discover that we find a way to receive the gift of our true self. We might find that we catch a glimpse of mystery, and like the disciples on the road to Emmaus, we too might say, "Were not our hearts burning within us while he was talking to us on the road, while he was opening the scriptures to us?" (Luke 24:32).

CHAPTER 8

A Well Within

Now when Jesus learned that the Pharisees had heard, "Jesus is making and baptizing more disciples than John"—although it was not Jesus himself but his disciples who baptized—he left Judea and started back to Galilee. But he had to go through Samaria. So he came to a Samaritan city called Sychar, near the plot of ground that Jacob had given to his son Joseph. Jacob's well was there, and Jesus, tired out by his journey, was sitting by the well. It was about noon.

A Samaritan woman came to draw water, and Jesus said to her, "Give me a drink." (His disciples had gone to the city to buy food.) The Samaritan woman said to him, "How is it that you, a Jew, ask a drink of me, a woman of Samaria?" (Jews do not share things in common with Samaritans.) Jesus answered her, "If you knew the gift of God, and who it is that is saying to you, 'Give me a drink,' you would have asked him, and he would have given you living water." The woman said to him, "Sir, you have no bucket, and the well is deep. Where do you get that living water? Are you greater than our ancestor Jacob, who gave us the well, and with his sons and his flocks drank from it?" Jesus said to her, "Everyone who drinks of this water will be thirsty again, but those who drink of the water that I will give them will never be thirsty. The water that I will give will become in them a spring of water gushing up to eternal life." The woman said to him, "Sir, give me this water, so that I may never be thirsty or have to keep coming here to draw water."

John 4:1–15

I was blessed with three children in less than three years. My first two children were born nineteen months apart and only fifteen months separate the second from the third. I was a stay-at-home mother until my youngest daughter started kindergarten and I began to attend Pittsburgh Theological Seminary. One of the things I remember clearly from the years I spent at home with my very small children is the time I spent in the basement doing laundry. Our basement is unfinished, has a cement floor, and has been described by my children as creepy. It is the home of many crawling insects, spiders, and thousand leggers, creatures that my daughter Rebecca claims come directly from hell. It is a cold, drab, rather unpleasant space. And yet, when my days upstairs were filled with demands from children who delighted me but who nevertheless needed a great deal of time, attention, and physical care, the moments I had sorting laundry in quiet and solitude were times that grabbed my attention, moments to stop, moments to breathe, moments of reflection, moments of grounding when I felt my pulse connected to something deeper than myself. It wasn't really like it sounds when I write it. I never looked forward to doing laundry. I didn't at the time recognize the spacious quality of those moments, but now looking back, I do remember the quiet washing over me, and with it a feeling of peace and a sense of God's presence.

The sense of God's presence I felt in the midst of those ordinary days surfaces in my memory as I think about the Samaritan woman encountering Jesus at Jacob's well. The Samaritan woman is in the midst of her ordinary day, at the well, filling jars with water to take home for cooking and for washing, when Jesus comes, sits down, asks her for a drink, and she finds herself in the midst of an encounter that will change her life forever. She moves from collecting water to take home, to a discussion of how and where to worship, to a recognition of Jesus as the Messiah, to eventually leaving her water jar behind to begin a new life as a disciple of Jesus, convincingly telling her story and leading others to Christ.[1] While my encounters with God's presence as I did laundry came in the form of a thin sound of silence, rather than a full-bodied conversation, and while the changes God's presence etched into my life came as slowly as the changes dripping water makes on a rock, nevertheless there is something in my encounter with God's presence in my basement that resembles the encounter between the Samaritan woman and Jesus. Their meeting at Jacob's well is not meant to merely inform us of a historical event in Jesus's life, but to teach us about our own encounters with Jesus at all the wells in our lives.

The story of the Samaritan woman is found in the Gospel of John. This is significant because John's Gospel tells readers the words, deeds, and life events of Jesus, but the focus of the telling is not on the surface manifestation of these events but on deeper ground lying below the events and filling them with meaning. The reader is invited to hear the events as an invitation to enter into their own encounter with Jesus and to find in this encounter their own experience of God's presence. Reflecting on interpreting scripture, Thomas Merton wrote, "What is hidden beneath the literal meaning is not merely another and more hidden meaning, it is also a new and totally different reality….It is the divine life itself."[2] Merton was referring to all of scripture, but this statement captures a truth that is essential if we are to listen deeply to the stories in the Gospel of John.

Because John's Gospel is intent on revealing hidden meaning, John uses symbolism to draw us toward a deeper encounter. Demetrius Dumm writes,

> In this way, not only human words, but also human persons and events, while remaining literal or historical, can be wonderfully enhanced by an added symbolic meaning. They become "larger than life" as they take on a universal and perennial meaning over and above their particular and time-bound significance. Thus, for example, when Jesus meets a Samaritan woman at Jacob's well, it is not just an interesting episode of ancient history. Rather, the "living water" which he offers her becomes an invitation to all subsequent hearers to abandon the stale well water of a purely natural existence and to accept Jesus' offer of fresh, living water which is the vibrant, exciting life of faith.[3]

The words of Merton and Dumm have led me to focus primarily on symbols in this story and to attempt to follow these symbols as they lead me to a life-giving encounter with Jesus. For this reason, I will let the symbols of well, light, and water guide us through our understanding of this story.

The first symbol we come to in the story is the well. Throughout scripture, wells are important meeting places. It was at a well that Isaac met Rebekah, Jacob met Rachel, and Moses met Zipporah, and in each case, the meeting at the well led to marriage. In our twenty-first century minds, marriage is about romance, but in the ancient world, these marriages united tribes, wed together peoples, not just the bride and the groom. Jesus and the Samaritan woman do not get married, but their meeting does point to a future in which these two groups of people, who are closely related and yet worship in different ways, will worship together in spirit and truth.[4] In the meetings of Isaac and Rebekah, Jacob and Rachel, and Moses and Zipporah, the intimate relationship between two people has significance for groups of people beyond them. So too, the intimate meeting between Jesus and the Samaritan woman has implications for the world beyond them.

The woman comes to draw water from the well at noon, the time of day when the light is at its fullest and brightest. The time is significant because the story of the Samaritan woman follows the story of Nicodemus. Nicodemus and the Samaritan woman are figures that are representative. Nicodemus represents the Pharisees and he comes to Jesus at night. Nicodemus, like the Pharisees he represents, is interested in Jesus but never fully understands or accepts him. The woman represents the Samaritans; she encounters Jesus when the light is the brightest and becomes convinced that he is the Messiah. Because of her encounter, many other Samaritans come to Jesus and receive him. From the opening of the Gospel, when it is said of Jesus the Word, "The light shines in the darkness, and the darkness did not overcome it" (1:5), to the closing of the Gospel when Jesus appears to his disciples "just after daybreak" (21:4), the Gospel associates light with God, life, and knowledge. The Samaritan woman meets Jesus at noon and receives the fullness of his light, life, and knowledge.

The woman comes to the well to draw water. It is a daily, ordinary task. Water is vital for drinking, for washing, for cooking, for life, and gathering water is a daily routine for people everywhere.[5] Water is a rich biblical symbol. In small gentle quantities, it is associated with quenching physical thirst, and metaphorically, it is tied to the revelation of God's presence that quenches our spiritual thirst for God. The Psalmist proclaims,

> O God, you are my God, I seek you,
>> my soul thirsts for you;
> my flesh faints for you,
>> as in a dry and weary land where there is no water.
> So I have looked upon you in the sanctuary,
>> beholding your power and glory.
> Because your steadfast love is better than life,
>> my lips will praise you.
>
> (Ps 63:1–3)

In the Old Testament and in rabbinic writings, water is associated with the law, with revelation, and with divine wisdom.[6] Water is a primary symbol in the first four chapters of the Gospel of John as well.[7] Jesus's baptism is not described in this Gospel but John the Baptist points out that while he baptizes in water, Jesus baptizes with the Holy Spirit (1:33). Jesus's first sign in the Gospel is to turn water into wine (2:1–12). Jesus tells Nicodemus that "no one can enter the kingdom of God without being born of water and Spirit" (3:5). And Jesus tells the Samaritan woman that he can give her living water, water that will become a spring of water within, water that leads to eternal life, water that will not simply quench current thirst but will result in never being thirsty again (4:13–14). Throughout the Gospel, Jesus transforms the ordinary but vital life-giving gift of water into something that exceeds time, place, and expectation.

The conversation Jesus and the Samaritan woman have at the well, like Psalm 63, links thirst, water, relationship with God, and worship together. Throughout their conversation attention is drawn to the issues that divide Jews from Samaritans. The conversation is initiated by Jesus, who asks the woman for a drink of water. The woman is surprised by his request and points out his social faux pas, "How is it that you, a Jew, ask a drink of me, a woman of Samaria?" Jews and Samaritans disagreed over issues of purity and where to worship. Jews sometimes considered Samaritans to be idolaters and accused them of intermarrying with the five nations that overtook them in the Assyrian invasion in 721 BC. A Jewish council adopted a ruling in AD 65–66 claiming Samaritan women as "menstruants from the cradle."[8] No wonder the Samaritan woman was surprised that Jesus asked her for a drink of water!

Jesus and the woman move from discussing water, to discussing her marriages, to whether it is proper to worship on Mt. Gerizim, the temple of the Samaritans, or in Jerusalem, the temple of the Jews. Jesus continually points toward revelation that transcends space and time. The discussion of water at one specific well points to living water that transcends geographic space and is always present. The woman's acceptance of Jesus's revelation leads to a discussion about the woman's five husbands. These husbands likely point to the history of the Samaritan people, invaded by five nations, and highlights the woman's role as a representative figure in the Gospel. Jesus shows his deep knowledge of the woman's past, and she understands he is a prophet. Their conversation turns to where to worship, a conversation that is once again rooted in the history of division between Jews and Samaritans. Jesus indicates that worship transcends geographic space, worship takes place in Spirit and truth; true worship is alive, flows from and is rooted in vibrant life-giving faith.

There is movement in the conversation between Jesus and the Samaritan woman. Jesus leads the woman to consider deeper and deeper aspects of her faith and to gradually more fully recognize who he is and what this means for her life. It is significant that he invites her to enter the spiritual life more deeply not by escaping her particularity but in and through it, through her own personal history, and through the history of her ancestors. As readers of the Gospel, we are invited to participate in this movement in our own lives. For most of us, this movement to deeper faith and to a fuller relationship with Jesus unfolds gradually over time. It is less a matter of one conversation at a well and more a matter of years and years of growing, maturing, and prayerfully practicing our faith. Looking back on my own life, I can see myself at the well and I can trace the moments of deepening faith, but the movement was very gradual, often confusing, and involved wearing out many pairs of sandals as I followed the winding path to that well for endless days over the course of many years.

My childhood home had a wonderful backyard. The yard was surrounded and separated from other yards and homes by tall pine trees on one side of the yard, and green, ordinary bushes on the other. The boundary at the back of the yard was formed by overgrown forsythia bushes that would awaken your hope after long, cold winters by bursting into beautiful spectacular yellow blossoms in the very early spring. There was a large tree in the center of the backyard in which I spent many hours of my childhood climbing and dwelling on its branches. I climbed so high in the tree once that I got stuck because I was afraid to come down. I discovered that when you are climbing up a tree and you reach for a branch just a little beyond you, it is exhilarating and fun, but when you are on the way down, that little extra space between the branch and your foot is terrifying. I had to wait high in the tree for some time until my father came home from work and patiently talked me down to the ground. Most of my childhood encounters with transcendence occurred when I was by myself in this backyard.

In this backyard, I learned about nature. I watched sunsets from my tree, rolled in the grass, watched ants build a nest, found pine cones, and made "soup" from dead pine needles, stirring them with a stick. In this backyard, I dreamed about my future. I read books and imagined myself in the pages of those books. I studied outside with the sun warming my back and knew that I would spend my life learning. My most profound encounter with transcendence is one that is difficult to describe. I was swinging on my backyard swing set, and as I was swinging, an awareness of peace and oneness overwhelmed me. I felt as though I was one with the sky, one with the rushing breeze, and part of the trees. The blue of the sky, the white of the clouds, the green of the grass and the trees became more vibrant as though lit from within. In that moment, I belonged to the world and the world was very beautiful and very good.

During the same early childhood years that I encountered transcendence in my backyard, I had other experiences of religion. My very best friend at that time was a girl named Rhonda who was the exact same age as me. Her house was just beyond the forsythia bushes, and we shared many happy times together in my backyard. I am not sure what denomination of Christian church her family belonged to, but one year they had a little mini Bible school on their front porch that I attended. The one thing I remember from this front-porch evangelization is that there was a lesson about how Jesus saves. The teacher used a poster-sized flip chart. She showed us a picture of a big black heart and told us that this is what our hearts currently looked like. She flipped to a picture of a clean, shining, white heart and told us that if we invited Jesus to come into our hearts, our hearts would turn white and God would come into our lives and through God's love we would be saved.

For some reason, this lesson had a profound effect on me. It was not hard to convince me that my heart was black, and I desperately wanted it to be white. I prayed fervently that Jesus would come into my heart. When I prayed, I would picture my heart turning white. The problem with this was that almost as soon as my prayer was over and I almost believed my heart was white so that God could love me, life would intrude and I would get into trouble, or make a mistake, and become convinced that my heart was once again black. I am sure the lesson that day sprang from good intentions and was meant to give me comfort in my salvation. Unfortunately, fed by the context of my life, it became a lesson that convinced me that I was incapable of ever being loved or saved.

I also experienced religion in a Presbyterian church that my family sporadically attended. Most of my early memories of church are memories of Easter services. The unspoken message I received as a child was that the importance of Easter church services lay entirely in my wearing spotless white gloves, shiny black patent leather shoes with a purse to match, and that I was to be quiet, sweet, and so well-behaved that not one hair would fall from my pretty new hair ribbon. The God we had come to worship was never mentioned. Unfortunately, my behavior always resulted in scuffed shoes, dirty white gloves, a lost hair ribbon, and disapproving looks from my mother. This, combined with the fact that despite my best efforts to be quiet and sweet, too many questions seemed to spill from my mouth, convinced me that there was something quite wrong with me.

The unspoken Easter service message resulted in my own twisted perception of the story of Easter. The story of Easter is one of sin and salvation, life and death. The idea that I was sinful seemed quite apparent. One look at my scuffed

shoes and at my mother's scornful glance convinced me of
this. That I needed salvation was obvious. But it was what
salvation would look like that became twisted in my mind.
I thought that salvation would result in my impressing the
people my mother so wanted me to impress, and in being
a quiet, sweet girl who never got dirty, or asked too many
questions.

For years I lived with this divide. I had profound encounters with God's presence in solitude in those moments in my
backyard, on long walks, on the beach, through the books
that I read, and in quiet moments of reflection, but all my
words about God, the language of religion, were associated
with judgment, associated with disapproval, associated with a
little black heart longing to be white. I think my first moment
of awakening at the well was that moment I walked into a
Catholic church in downtown Johnstown when I was twelve.
It was because no one was talking that this moment was so
profound. There were symbols, there was darkness, there were
candles, there was a crucifix, and there was silence. Silence
drew me to the Catholic Church and the ritual of the liturgy
deepened my encounter with that silence. In the mystery of
that silence, the words about God, the language of religion,
slowly began to weave themselves together with my experiences of God's presence in solitude. It is only in and through
this weaving that I was able to begin to worship in Spirit and
truth, to draw life from worship, to begin to live from faith,
to begin to experience wholeness in my being and oneness in
my faith. I continue to listen in silence and silence continues
to ground me in mystery, weaving together words with experience, stirring in me an awareness of the intimacy of God's
presence in every moment of my life, teaching me that I will
not find God by going out, nor by going to a specific place,
nor by praying specific words, but in and through my very
own self in the daily experience of my life, and by awakening

to the daily gifts of "love, joy, peace, patience, kindness, generosity, faithfulness, gentleness, and self-control" (Gal 5:22–23).

My favorite verse in the story of the Samaritan woman is when she addresses Jesus with these words, "Sir, you have no bucket, and the well is deep. Where do you get that living water?" (John 4:11). Jesus is offering her eternal life, and she is worried that he doesn't have a bucket! This humorous verse is profoundly meaningful. Her misunderstanding of Jesus shows us how difficult it is to listen to, and for, the thin sound of God in the silence. We spend so much time and energy on the surface of life. Some of that time and energy is necessary because we do have to take care of our physical and psychological needs in this life. But when we allow ourselves to get lost in the anxiety of the physical and psychological dimensions of life, when we forget to be quiet, to listen, to allow the deeper mystery of life to penetrate our being, we can find ourselves circling and circling around the same problems over and over again, thirsting for a solution but unable to find water.

Jesus tells the woman, "Everyone who drinks of this water will be thirsty again, but those who drink of the water that I will give them will never be thirsty. The water that I will give will become in them a spring of water gushing up to eternal life" (4:13–14). Jesus's response to the Samaritan woman asks me to trust. It tells me to stop working so hard to solve problems I do not understand. My efforts to solve these problems only results in speech that increases in intensity as it races across the surface but will never lead me to a deeper place. Instead, I am asked to receive the gift of water, to open my heart, to listen in silence. Increasingly I have come to long for, to love, to nurture silence, because in that silent space, my words about God gradually begin to be woven together with my experience of God's presence, and as this happens, I hear hints of running, living water and begin to hope that I might continue to live more firmly rooted and with ever-deepening trust in the source of this life-giving water.

Give us the inner listening that is a way in itself and the oldest thirst there is.

—Rumi

CHAPTER 9

Attending to Emptiness

> When it was evening, there came a rich man from
> Arimathea, named Joseph, who was also a disciple of
> Jesus. He went to Pilate and asked for the body of Jesus;
> then Pilate ordered it to be given to him. So Joseph
> took the body and wrapped it in a clean linen cloth and
> laid it in his own new tomb, which he had hewn in the
> rock. He then rolled a great stone to the door of the
> tomb and went away. Mary Magdalene and the other
> Mary were there, sitting opposite the tomb.
>
> Matthew 27:57–61

Every semester, I teach two sections of a course called First Theology. This is a required course for St. Vincent College students, and most of the students enrolled in the course are freshman. On the final exam, I give students a bonus question. The question is, What do you think is the most significant thing you learned in this class and why? This past semester, I received the following answer:

> The most significant thing I learned in class was
> that no one fully understands God and that it is

impossible to have a clear knowledge of who He is. I think this is most significant because I have honestly struggled with faith, since I didn't understand God. I asked a lot of questions we addressed in class such as how does God explain innocent suffering? However, by discussing the fact that there is no right answer to many questions it has helped me to realize I will never truly understand God and that is okay. By accepting this truth I feel much better about my lack of understanding. As a result I feel more compelled to accept God for the mystery that He is. This has really improved my relationship with God and the role I want Him to play in my life.[1]

This answer highlights the significant role questions play in a life of faith. Authentic faith does not allow certitude to close our hearts to the ambiguity, vulnerability, and pain of our human condition. We are people who "sit in darkness and in the shadow of death" (Luke 1:79). We may hope or trust that daybreak will visit us from on high. We may even live as though daybreak is our entire reality, but somewhere buried beneath our best attempts at optimism is the reality that each one of us will one day die, that our treasured loved ones will die, that we will likely feel overwhelmed by darkness at some point in our lives, and that there is suffering in the world that we cannot understand or explain. Faith has to begin with acknowledging this reality, facing our human limitations, facing the reality of our vulnerability. Faith must be able to wait through a long, dark night, facing the tomb, facing the sadness, emptiness, and questions of meaninglessness that tombs evoke, and yet allowing ourselves to be guided on a path of peace by a light we trust is present even when we cannot see it clearly or understand its mystery. Faith is allowing our questions and the limits of our knowledge to awaken us to the wonder of the Mystery that is God and draw us more deeply into love.

At the empty tomb of Jesus, we come face-to-face with mystery, mystery that eludes the power structures of the world. Matthew's account of the empty tomb is my favorite because it highlights the efforts of both Rome and the religious authorities to control the events that unfold and the complete failure of their attempts. The chief priests and the Pharisees ask Pilate for a guard because they remember that Jesus had talked about rising from the dead in three days. They wanted to make sure that Jesus's body was in the tomb, proving Jesus wrong, and completely defeating his movement. So Pilate agrees and stations guards at the tomb, and even seals the very large, immovable stone at the entrance to the tomb. Even after the tomb is discovered empty, the guards are bribed to say that Jesus's disciples stole the body during the night.

Despite the efforts of those in authority to control events, the sealed stone is moved by an angel of the Lord and the women find the tomb empty. In all four Gospels, women are the primary witnesses of Jesus's crucifixion and the first to discover the empty tomb. This is significant because in the first-century world and in many places in the world today, women are not part of the power structures in their societies. One consequence of this is that women are often the ones who attend most fully to the aspects of life least able to be manipulated and controlled. Women are the primary caretakers, nurturers, and witnesses to those on the boundaries of life, to those who are being born, and those who are dying. Women are often the ones who sit down and face the tomb.

The stationing of guards, the attempt to secure the tomb, and the buying of false witnesses is reminiscent of the attempt of Pharaoh to control the Hebrew slaves at the beginning of Exodus. He first attempts to work them so hard that they will stop multiplying. When this doesn't work, he orders the Hebrew midwives to kill the male babies when they are born. When this doesn't work, he orders all male babies to be thrown into the Nile. In the first chapters of Exodus, it is also women who attend to the birth, women who assure the future of the baby Moses, and women who operate from the margins but nevertheless thwart the power structures of Egypt.

These two stories point to the power and mystery of God to overturn expectations and to elude the control of those who think they are in power in the world. In both stories, the women do not control the events that unfold, but they attend to the needs of the moment. They listen to the demands of life in the midst of death. They won't stifle the cry of the newborn babies. They won't throw Moses into the river without a basket. Even the Pharaoh's daughter is unable to let the baby Moses die, but instead draws him from the water. The women who face the tomb are also attentive to the demands of life. They do not leave Jesus alone to die. They do not leave his tomb unattended. They bring spices to the tomb to anoint his body. Their presence at the cross, their willingness to face the tomb through a long, dark night, their attention to the gesture of anointing the body of Jesus shows their love and respect for the life of Jesus. It is clear that the death of Jesus is beyond their control, but they will do what they can, they will attend to his body, and by attending to his body, they will enter into relationship with the mystery of his death.

As I write this chapter, the reality of death is a fresh experience for me because my father passed away less than one month ago. The experience of my father's death is too new for me to have found a reflective space separate from the emotions of loss. The experience is still very raw. But maybe my inability to be free from the emotions of loss, my experience in the morass of the darkness that comes with grief, will allow me to speak of what I have encountered through my father's death. What I have encountered is a deepening of mystery. I do not have clarity about the meaning of my father's death. I do not even think I understand much about my father. But I do have peace. I do have a sense of spaciousness and the presence of God and a sense that my father is at peace despite my inability to understand the experience or know much about my father's interior life.

Forty years ago, when I was in middle school (it was called junior high school then), we discussed death in a health class. I remember the teacher writing all the factors of life that might lead to an early death on the board. The list included family history of early death, smoking, excessive consumption of coffee, excessive consumption of alcohol, stressful job, and sleeping less than eight hours a night. From the moment that list went up on the board until my father's recent death, I was keenly aware that my father was going to die. My father's father was in his fifties when he died of a heart attack. My father smoked two packs of cigarettes a day, drank alcohol every night, and stayed up until 1:00 in the morning. He then got up four or five hours later to drink a pot of coffee before he left for his very stressful management job at Bethlehem Steel. The list on the blackboard in my health class awakened me to the inevitable mortality of my father. From that moment of awakening, I never said goodbye to my father without a whisper that told me to appreciate him in that moment because I may never see him again. The list on the blackboard oriented me to face his tomb.

Like any middle school child confronted with this information, I felt it was my duty to convince my father to change the way he lived his life. I campaigned for him to quit smoking, quit drinking coffee, quit consuming alcohol, and to go to bed earlier. My father found my attempts to reform his life amusing. He told me on many occasions that he was satisfied with whatever length of life he was given, that he intended to live every day he was given the way he wanted to live it, and that he would rather live fully in the small amount of time he was given than to live with constant watchfulness and worry about extending his days. He lived much longer than either one of us expected, and I think the only years he disliked were the last two or three years when health issues forced him to live a small life restricted by the limitations his failing body imposed upon him.

The interesting thing about my awakening to the mortality of my father is that when my father died, it did not feel tragic to me. All those years of facing the tomb had formed a space within me to accept my father's inevitable passing from this life and had given me the chance to know his feelings about it. My father was not an overtly religious man. He did not go to church, pray, or talk about God, and yet he was extremely loving, kind, and accepting. He was humble. He stayed in the background. He was a person of integrity. He knew who he was, accepted both his faults and his gifts, and because of this acceptance, warmly welcomed and accepted other people. He did not need life to be perfect, but received the gifts life offered him with gratitude. I was one of the gifts he received, and he let me know how much this gift meant to him not through his words, but through the way he treated me. I could hear his delight in me, his joy about my being, his acceptance of me with all my faults and gifts in the way he said hello to me when he recognized my voice on the phone. I hope I will always remember the warmth in his voice welcoming me as he greeted me on the phone. When my father died, I wrote his eulogy. Writing the eulogy helped me to think about how little I knew about many aspects of my father's life and, at the same time, how deeply I knew him. I know who my father was in a way I know few other people. I know what is essential about my father; know him in the depths of my self, in my habits, in my attitudes, in my tendencies, and in my own acceptance of both the limitations and gifts life offers.

I imagine Mary Magdalene and Mary, the mother of James and Joseph, the women who sat through a long, dark night facing the tomb, thought a lot about who Jesus was, how much they did not know or understand about him, and yet how deeply they knew him. The death of Jesus was not like the death of my father. It did not come at the end of a full life, but was a violent upheaval that ripped through the souls of his followers and overturned the ground on which they stood. But when you are facing the tomb, your own or the tomb of someone you know, complexity falls away and what is essential comes to the surface. Perhaps what came to the surface for these women, what they found to be essential amid the confusion of their last few days, was who Jesus was, whom they knew him to be as they followed him on the way, the essential aspects of Jesus's incarnation that Matthew highlights from the very beginning of his Gospel.

When Joseph finds out that Mary is pregnant, he knows the child is not his and considers leaving. He is visited by an angel of the Lord and is told that the child is from the Holy Spirit and that he should take Mary into his home and raise the child as his own. At that time, the angel tells Joseph to name the baby Jesus. The name Jesus was Greek for the Hebrew *Yeshua*, a name popularly known to be related to the Hebrew verb *to save* and the noun *salvation*.[2] Throughout the Old Testament, the Hebrew verb *to save* is used to indicate rescue from physical danger of some kind, from enemies, from prison, from injustice, from sickness.[3] Salvation could also indicate forgiveness of sins, and Matthew tells us that Jesus will be known as one who saves "for he will save his people from their sins" (1:21). This explanation in Matthew indicates that the saving character of Jesus will be revealed not in the realm of liberation from the politics of oppression but in the personal realm. Liberation will remove the wall that sin, sickness, and death have created between God and human beings. Toward the end of the Gospel, the forgiveness of sins is tied to Jesus's own death when his lifeblood is poured out for the forgiveness of sins (26:28).[4] Even before Jesus is born, Matthew points his readers toward Jesus's tomb.

As Joseph is told that the baby will be named Jesus, he is also told that Jesus will fulfill a prophecy (1:22–23). Through the fulfillment of this prophecy Jesus will be called Emmanuel. This is not necessarily the name Mary and Joseph will use to call their son, but a title that will help all of us understand the meaning of Jesus, who he was in his life and who he is through his resurrection. The name Emmanuel means "God is with us." Matthew's Gospel opens with reference to Jesus as the presence of God with us and his Gospel closes with the promise of Jesus's continuing presence: "And remember, I am with you always, to the end of the age" (28:20).

These two essential aspects of Jesus's identity, that he is the one who saves and that he is the presence of God with us, must have surfaced in the minds and hearts of Mary Magdalene and the other Mary as they sat in the dark and looked at the sealed stone, a stone they could not possibly move, a stone that, like death, separated them from the person of Jesus. As they sat in the dark, this must have posed a mystery for them. How could the one who was to save them, how could the one who was to be the presence of God with us, be lying dead in a tomb? How could life come from this situation of death? And yet they stayed there through the night, through the silence, through the dark, and they came to the tomb in the morning as though they would be able to move that stone. They didn't understand but they knew. They knew Jesus and they trusted that despite the presence of guards, and bribes, and attempts to kill and oppress Jesus and his message, the essence of Jesus as the one who saves and the presence of God remained. The women accepted this gift without understanding it and did what they could, attended to life in the midst of death, attended to emptiness without finding it meaningless, attended to emptiness as a form of spaciousness that might bring to light new life.

Matthew makes it clear in his Gospel that the mystery of Jesus precedes his birth and continues after his death; mystery encompasses the life of Jesus. In fact, mystery encompasses all our lives. Some moments of life, particularly birth and death, compel us to face this mystery. Perhaps we are more comfortable with the mystery of birth because it is a beginning. We can move from the beginning of life to nurturing the life we have received as a gift. We can more easily identify tasks that we can manipulate and control. Death is harder though. Death confronts us more fully with our lack of control. Death is never planned, it comes to us, interrupts our lives, demands that we stop ordinary life and pay attention to the silence that we do not understand. Of course our faith tells us to hope for, in fact to expect, the resurrection from the dead, but hoping for this, believing in this does not take away the loss of the relationship we knew with the person who has died. Yet paradoxically, facing the tomb is essential if we are going to fully receive the gifts of life we are given.

St. Benedict recognized the importance of facing death for living a full life. In chapter four of *The Rule of Benedict*, a chapter entitled, "The Tools for Good Works," Benedict writes, "Yearn for everlasting life with holy desire. Day by day remind yourself that you are going to die. Hour by hour keep careful watch over all you do, aware that God's gaze is upon you, wherever you may be." Benedict's admonition is not meant to lead us to despair and sadness but to the purpose of our lives. We are to recognize that our life comes from God and belongs to God. We are reminded that the way we come to know the presence of God is in and through the lives we live. Our task in life is to "love the Lord your God with all your heart, and with all your soul, and with all your mind.... [and] love your neighbor as yourself" (Matt 22:37–39; see also Mark 12:30–31; Luke 10:27), verses Benedict uses to open the chapter. We do this by attending to the needs of the people around us, relieving the lot of the poor, clothing the naked, visiting the sick, burying the dead, helping the troubled, and consoling the sorrowing.[5] Our awareness of the mystery of God deepens when we attend to the aspects of life of which we are least in control, aspects of life that open within us awareness of suffering, emptiness, meaninglessness, and death. When we attend faithfully to these aspects of life, we may find that there are many events in life, many dimensions of people, and many questions about God we will never fully understand, and yet through our faithful attention to these aspects of life, we come to accept, know, and love God more deeply. As people who sit in darkness and the shadow of death, attending to emptiness carves out a space within us to receive God's love.

Theologian and writer Frederick Buechner writes,

> Part of the inner world of everyone is this sense of emptiness, unease, incompleteness, and I believe that this in itself is a word from God, that this is the sound that God's voice makes in a world that explains him away. In such a world, I suspect that maybe God speaks to us most clearly through his silence, his absence, so that we know him best through our missing him.[6]

If we miss our emptiness, if we run from it, if we live consistently distracted by tasks we can manipulate and control, tasks that win us power and recognition in the world but fail us when we come to the tomb, we miss our yearning for God. We miss the mystery that gives us life and calls us home. We miss the spaciousness that emptiness carves within us in order for love to make its home in us (John 15:4).[7]

CHAPTER 10

Daybreak

Early on the first day of the week, while it was still dark, Mary Magdalene came to the tomb and saw that the stone had been removed from the tomb. So she ran and went to Simon Peter and the other disciple, the one whom Jesus loved, and said to them, "They have taken the Lord out of the tomb, and we do not know where they have laid him." Then Peter and the other disciple set out and went toward the tomb. The two were running together, but the other disciple outran Peter and reached the tomb first. He bent down to look in and saw the linen wrappings lying there, but he did not go in. Then Simon Peter came, following him, and went into the tomb. He saw the linen wrappings lying there, and the cloth that had been on Jesus' head, not lying with the linen wrappings but rolled up in a place by itself. Then the other disciple, who reached the tomb first, also went in, and he saw and believed; for as yet they did not understand the scripture, that he must rise from the dead. Then the disciples returned to their homes.

But Mary stood weeping outside the tomb. As she wept, she bent over to look into the tomb; and she saw two angels in white, siting where the body of Jesus had been lying, one at the head and the other at the feet. They said to her, "Woman, why are you weeping?" She said to them, "They have taken away my Lord, and I do not know where they have laid him." When she had said this, she turned around and saw Jesus standing there, but she did not know that it was Jesus. Jesus said to her, "Woman, why are you weeping? Whom are you looking for?" Supposing him to be the gardener, she said to him, "Sir, if you have carried him away, tell me where you have laid him, and I will take him away." Jesus said to her, "Mary!" She turned and said to him in Hebrew, "Rabbouni!" (which means Teacher). Jesus said to her "Do not hold on to me, because I have not yet ascended to the Father. But go to my brothers and say to them, 'I am ascending to my Father and your Father, to my God and your God.'" Mary Magdalene went and announced to the disciples, "I have seen the Lord"; and she told them that he had said these things to her.

John 20:1–18

There is an oil painting that hangs in my office. The painting depicts three male disciples on a hill above the city of Jerusalem, carrying a large cloth holding the dead body of Jesus. Behind the male disciples, four women follow. One of the women is Mary Magdalene, whose face is hidden because she is weeping. Her face is in her hands and both her hands and face are surrounded by beautiful, long, flowing hair. This scene was painted by my mother-in-law, Evelyn Sharbaugh, and given to me as a gift when I graduated from Pittsburgh Theological Seminary in 1999.

My mother-in-law is a wonderful artist. She graduated from Carnegie Mellon University with a degree in art, taught for a brief moment, and then packed her paints and canvasses away for a time as she became the mother of nine children. Only ten and a half years separate the oldest of the nine from the youngest. My husband, John, told me two stories about Evie that capture the playfulness and creativity of his mother. The first is that when the children were all young, his mother would sometimes transform a mundane task, like washing hair, into a creative, playful opportunity. On occasion, all the children would line up in front of the kitchen sink and one by one step up to lean over and get their hair washed. Evie would shampoo their hair and with the soap still in their hair, sculpt the hair and bubbles into an artistic design. One by one they would then leave the sink with their dripping heads to check out their head sculptures in a mirror, get back in line and step up to have the shampoo rinsed from their heads.

The second story John told me is that they had a very old refrigerator that looked worn and dilapidated. To spruce it up, John's mother would allow the children to paint on the refrigerator. They would paint whatever they wanted to, an animal, a house, a scene from nature; then while they were sleeping, his mother would go back and embellish their painting, making it come to life, giving it an artistic touch-up so that their young attempt at painting became a masterpiece. She did this in a way that included them, made them feel special; put them in touch with their own deeply hidden artistic ability. My mother-in-law is very playful, and she made life joyful for her children even though she, herself, often felt exhausted.

While Evie was painting the scene that hangs in my office, she had in front of her a painting that was in her Bible and depicted a similar scene. In the painting she used as the basis for the one she did for me, Mary Magdalene is weeping as in mine, but her dress is also hanging off of her shoulder, symbolizing the false but common belief that Mary Magdalene was a prostitute who was forgiven and healed from her moral depravity by Jesus. Evie had attended a class I taught about the biblical Mary Magdalene and had, therefore, painted her in a modest dress that covered her shoulders and depicted her as a grieving but respectable woman.

As any theologian knows, determining the historical person that lies behind the biblical text is difficult business. This is true for all biblical figures and yet seems to be even more difficult when Mary Magdalene is the subject. Within the first four entries that surface when I type "Mary Magdalene" into the library catalogue at St. Vincent College is one book entitled *Invoking Mary Magdalene: Accessing the Wisdom of the Divine Feminine* and another book called *The Life of St. Mary Magdalene: Or, the Path of Penitence*. These two entries represent the polarization of much of the research and popular interest in Mary Magdalene. Older books depict Mary Magdalene as the ultimate sinner, and contemporary scholarship sometimes tries to correct this misunderstanding by moving in a direction that paints her either as a divine feminine wisdom figure, or as the lover or wife of Jesus. There seems to be reluctance to see Mary Magdalene as she most likely was, a woman healed by Jesus who became a dedicated disciple, following him, learning from him, and providing for his mission, a mission she believed in, a mission focused on bringing the kingdom of God into the world through healing the sick, casting out demons, freeing captives, and bringing good news to the poor.

Trying to understand who Mary Magdalene really was, the nature of her relationship with Jesus, and what her role was as a leader in the early church involves digging through layers of accumulated misunderstandings that cling to her like barnacles on a ship, making it difficult to see her and almost impossible to know her. This is a particularly interesting problem in light of the biblical text in John's Gospel. Because at the heart of this text, Jesus calls Mary by name, she recognizes his voice, and she knows herself because she is known by him. Her identity is rooted in her relationship with Jesus, and that relationship is formative for all of Christianity, for in and through this relationship Mary becomes the apostle to the apostles, announcing, "I have seen the Lord."

This story highlights for us the importance of finding our true selves, the selves that awaken when Jesus calls to us, that know Jesus's voice. The treatment of Mary Magdalene in the history of interpretation shows us how quickly external voices, the voices of other people in the world, are willing and able to invade, distort, and cover over the truth of whom we are called to be and the challenge we face in listening and discerning the truth that lies beneath other people's false and distorting labels and interpretations of us. Reading this story helps us to reflect on how difficult it can be to listen and hear the voice of the good shepherd calling us by name, and reveals the great hope for our lives when we learn to hear that voice.

What we know about Mary Magdalene from the Bible is that she was an important disciple of Jesus. In all four Gospels she is named as one of the women who witness the crucifixion and as the one who discovers the empty tomb. In Mark, Matthew, and Luke, she discovers the empty tomb with other women. In John, she is accompanied by Peter and the beloved disciple. She is named first when she is listed with other women and is also named before Peter and the beloved disciple in John's Gospel. Naming her first indicates that she was considered to be a leader. In all four Gospels she is given the task of telling the apostles that Jesus had been raised from the dead. This leads to her being called the apostle to the apostles.[1]

Further information about Mary Magdalene is given to us in Luke's Gospel. His Gospel tells us,

> Soon afterwards he went on through cities and villages, proclaiming and bringing the good news of the kingdom of God. The twelve were with him, as well as some women who had been cured of evil spirits and infirmities: Mary, called Magdalene, from whom seven demons had gone out, and Joanna, the wife of Herod's steward Chuza, and Susanna, and many others, who provided for them out of their resources. (Luke 8:1–3)

From this passage we know that Mary was from a small town in Galilee and Jesus healed her of some illness that had a complete hold on her physically, emotionally, and psychologically. In the Bible, seven is associated with completion or perfection.[2] Her illness is unclear. Many commentators associate it with mental illness, but the important thing to note is that it was an illness; the demons are not associated with moral depravity in any way. Nowhere in the Bible is Mary referred to as a sinner or as a prostitute.[3] After being healed, Mary traveled with Jesus and the Twelve and some other women, and all of these women served or provided for Jesus's ministry. The verb used for serving or providing is the same Greek word that is used in connection with Peter's mother-in-law and implies a form of ministry (see chapter 5).

One thing that stood out for me when I was reading and thinking about Mary Magdalene is that apart from the account of her encounter with Jesus in a garden in John's Gospel, she is always listed with others. She travels with a group who are with Jesus. She goes to the empty tomb with others. Furthermore, when she addresses Jesus in John's Gospel, she calls him *Rabbouni*, teacher, a title that points to a relationship of formation that is personal and yet related to learning about God, the world, the kingdom of God, and one's relationship to it. I find this interesting because so much that is written about Mary Magdalene, so much of the misinterpretation of her, is focused on a very personal relationship with Jesus that does not remain on the level of friendship or teacher/disciple, but hints at something more, a relationship seasoned with erotic undertones.

Misinterpretation of the biblical text occurred when Mary Magdalene's story, either through neglect, lack of concern for women, or perhaps an intentional need to subordinate women, became confused and conflated with two other gospel stories. Rather than understand the three stories as referring to three different women, interpreters blended the three women into one. This is how Mary of Magdala came to be associated with the sinful woman in chapter 7 of Luke's Gospel, and with the anointing of Jesus by Mary of Bethany in John, chapter 12. Through this confused interpretation, a composite picture of Mary Magdalene was formed, and she became the ultimate sinner, a prostitute whom Jesus saved from her great sin. Mary's reputation as a great sinner, as a penitent follower of Jesus dominated popular imagination for centuries. Contemporary biblical scholarship and theologians have written, preached, and taught about the need to revise this understanding, but Mary Magdalene's reputation as a prostitute continues to be propagated in movies, artwork, and imaginative works about Jesus.[4]

The tradition of Mary Magdalene as a prostitute and great sinner is not the only misinterpretation of her relationship to Jesus. In a bestselling book by Henry Lincoln, *The Holy Blood and the Holy Grail*, Jesus and Mary Magdalene are lovers, have a daughter, and their descendants are associated with a dynasty of kings. According to this book, descendants of Mary and Jesus are still alive in Europe today. Dan Brown draws from this legend and popularizes it in his bestselling book, *The Da Vinci Code*.[5]

These distortions of Mary Magdalene are so prevalent, move so far from the biblical text, and concentrate so much on personal relationships laced with sensuality and sexuality, that we must recognize the role gender plays in these misrepresentations. Peter denies Jesus three times and yet Mary Magdalene, not Peter, is depicted as the ultimate sinner.[6] Peter was married and had a mother-in-law, but very little time or energy is spent reflecting on Peter's personal relationships. Unfortunately, the tendency to see women only in light of their personal relationships—in their roles as wives, mothers, daughters, and lovers—and then to use their personal relationship as fuel for false accusations of promiscuity is both ancient and enduring. Furthermore, not only does the association of women's reputations with the realm of the deeply personal provide a challenge for women to be seen as leaders in public roles, but it leaves them open to criticism for any behavior that might be interpreted as promiscuous or threatening to the deeply personal roles with which women are primarily identified.

Using the external reputation of a woman as a means of judging her character has deep and ancient roots. We can see these roots in this passage from the Wisdom of Ben Sira (Ecclesiasticus), written in the early years of the second century BC:

> A daughter is a secret anxiety to her father,
>   and worry over her robs him of sleep;
> when she is young, for fear she may not marry,
>   or if married, for fear she may be disliked;
> while a virgin, for fear she may be seduced
>   and become pregnant in her father's house;

or having a husband, for fear she my go astray,
    or, though married, for fear she may be barren.
Keep strict watch over a headstrong daughter,
    or she may make you a laughingstock to your
        enemies,
a byword in the city and the assembly of the
        people,
    and put you to shame in public gatherings.
See that there is no lattice in her room,
    no spot that overlooks the approaches to the
        house.
Do not let her parade her beauty before any man,
    or spend her time among married women;
for from garments comes the moth,
    and from a woman comes woman's wickedness.
Better is the wickedness of a man than a woman
    who does good;
    it is a woman who brings shame and disgrace.
                  (Sir 42:9–14)[7]

Notice how the daughter's reputation is drawn entirely from how her relationship with others is perceived and not from any internal qualities of character. The woman is judged by many things that are beyond her control. She can be maligned because she is infertile, or because she is beautiful, or because there is even an appearance of impropriety. With these cultural assumptions about women and the demands they place on women's behavior, it is not difficult to see how and why Mary of Magdala came to be judged on imagined impropriety and why interpretations of her story were so focused on her fictional past as a prostitute or on a relationship with Jesus laced with sensuality.[8] Very few interpreters consider that maybe Mary Magdalene followed Jesus because she cared deeply about his mission and wanted to participate in and see the changes his mission could bring to the world.

Even though women today are valued for their achievements, are educated, hold positions of status, and are recognized as leaders outside of the home, the long history of sexism and patriarchy continues to shape women's lives. The constraints and fears expressed in Sirach are no longer as extreme, but their remnants can be seen and heard not only in external evaluations of women but woven within and through women's internal understanding of themselves as well. Women still carry within themselves a heightened self-consciousness about how they will be judged and viewed by others.

One example of this comes to mind. I have a friend, Caroline, who attended seminary with me and now lives in New York City. Caroline has earned an MDiv and a PhD, and is an ordained Presbyterian minister. A few years ago, she organized a conference on violence and religion. The planning and development of this conference took several years. When the conference was held, it was recognized in national papers and journals. In one of the publications, I came across a picture of Caroline sitting on a panel between two men, one a rabbi and the other a Roman Catholic priest. I sent an email to Caroline congratulating her on the success of the conference. I praised her fortitude, perseverance, organizational skills, and intelligence in pulling together this successful, well-received conference. The last thing I mentioned in the email was that I thought the dress and scarf she was wearing in the picture were lovely and she looked really beautiful. Her immediate response was, "I don't have time to tell you about the conference right now, but thank you so much for saying that you liked my dress! When I bought the dress, I thought it was really pretty, but then I began to think that maybe it would be seen as unprofessional, maybe I should have worn a suit." Even though Caroline is an extremely accomplished, professional woman, she still has great anxiety that she might be judged, labeled, seen as somehow inappropriate, misunderstood, and misinterpreted because of what she wears. I think this is a normal, recognizable anxiety that plagues women to a far greater degree than men.

The story of Mary's encounter with Jesus in the garden of resurrection is a story that can teach us something about listening more deeply and allowing ourselves to be re-created amid distorted external and internal expectations. In the book *Beloved Disciple*, Robin Griffith-Jones states that the garden where Jesus's tomb lies is a place of death but is also the place of new life, and for that reason, every expectation is about to be overturned.[9] Griffith-Jones also points out that the Gospel of John invites its readers to enter the transformation. Readers have been undergoing transformation throughout the Gospel and are prepared to be Mary Magdalene at the end.[10] I am going to take this invitation seriously as I seek to find meaning in the encounter between Jesus and Mary Magdalene in the garden of resurrection.

Mary comes to the tomb on the first day of the week, while it is still dark. Matthew tells us she comes as the first day is dawning and Luke tells us it is daybreak (Matt 28:1; Luke 24:1). She comes while it is still dark, but by the time she converses with Jesus, there is clearly enough light for her to see him. She moves in this story from darkness to light. Her initial darkness is not simply about arriving before the sun; her darkness is the darkness of grief, the grief of losing a friend, mentor, and healer. Perhaps it is also about a lack of understanding, confusion about what has happened, a confusion that is exacerbated by the mysterious empty tomb and missing body of Jesus. Mary expresses her confusion to Peter and the beloved disciple and restates it to the two angels she sees sitting at the head and feet of Jesus, "They have taken away my Lord, and I do not know where they have laid him" (John 20:13).

Amid Mary's confusion, she mistakes the risen Christ for the gardener. Her confusion dissipates immediately, however, when Jesus calls her name, "Mary!" She responds at once, "Rabbouni." Mary's recognition of Jesus's voice recalls Jesus's instruction that the sheep will recognize the voice of the good shepherd (see John 10). It is a poignant moment. The intimate encounter between Jesus and Mary speaks to our experience because we know what it is like to have this instantaneous, deep recognition when someone calls our name, how deeply a loved one's voice resonates in our hearts, how immediate our response, how in the best circumstances that voice awakens us to ourselves and calls us home.

It is worth pausing briefly here to consider the many circumstances and ways in which we are called and recognize our names. Some of these recognitions take place in the rich soil of love and freedom, bringing comfort and warm feelings of home. Others bring with them the complex emotions that surface when our names are called in the midst of relationships that are threatening to our inner lives, while still others call us toward a future self that is deeper and richer than we ever thought possible.

My first job out of college was working as an accountant (my undergraduate degree was in accounting) for an international ball bearing company. I was trained for this job by a man named Lorenzo. Lorenzo was an interesting person, unique, different, quite unexpected. He was a character. Lorenzo was in his forties, had never left home, and lived with his mother. He took a vacation every year to Las Vegas, and memories of past vacations or dreams about the next vacation occupied a prevalent place in his conversations. He was tall, very thin, and could walk incredibly fast with a full mug of coffee without spilling one drop. He would mutter to himself throughout the day saying things like, "Sometimes you eat the bear; sometimes the bear eats you."

For some reason, even though Lorenzo had a new job, he seemed to resent handing over his old job to me. So when he taught me how to do something, he always moved and talked far too quickly for me to understand. His teaching was always incomplete, and he never waited to see if I understood. One of the tasks Lorenzo handed off to me was a spreadsheet that reported the daily sales of ball bearings. After several months of working and preparing the daily sales sheet, I had an abscessed tooth and had to miss a day of work. Because of my absence, Lorenzo was given the task of completing the spreadsheet that day. When I returned to work the next day, my coworkers told me that as Lorenzo was preparing the spreadsheet, he was constantly muttering and shaking his head back and forth saying, "Patty, Patty, Patty, Patty, Patty," with the clear implication that I had really fouled up the entire system.

Lorenzo is just one example, an example more humorous than threatening, of someone who used my name in a way that really had nothing to do with who I am as a person. If Lorenzo called my name today, I would not recognize his voice and no part of me would respond to his call, but there are those who might call my name and awaken very destructive feelings, feelings that feed distortions of my understanding of self, like thoughts that I am a liar, a coward, and generally a very disappointing person. The problem with this is that there is a deep part of myself that will still respond to these allegations even if they do misrepresent who I am. These distortions and labels have impacted my interior world, and the residue of bad feeling they produce is always lying dormant within me waiting to be fed. Sometimes these dormant feelings are fed and spring up quickly, taking life within me and coloring my world for days at a time. It is then that like Mary Magdalene, I am waiting in the darkness, weeping and peering into the empty tomb.

It is not simple or easy to hear our names in a way that helps us to recognize who we are and the purpose and meaning of our lives. Like Mary Magdalene, we can get lost in the darkness of confusion when we run up against the forces in the world that point toward death, forces that sometimes begin outside ourselves but often become part of our interior world as well. What this story in John's Gospel tells us, though, is that even while we wait in darkness, we have great hope. We may not know it yet, but even as we weep, we are living in the midst of daybreak, daybreak that comes because Jesus has identified himself with us.

Jesus begins his conversation with Mary by asking her two questions: "Why are you weeping?" and "For whom are you looking?" The first question reminds us of the deep compassion of Jesus. The second is very similar to a question Jesus asks two disciples in the first chapter of John: "What are you looking for?" (1:38). In John's Gospel, the answer to the question, what or who are you looking for, is always Jesus. It is Jesus who gives life, light, and the power to become children of God (1:1–18). In the beginning of the Gospel, the disciples are invited to come and see where Jesus is staying, and the Gospel tells us that they did go to where Jesus was staying and remained with him that day (1:39). They come to know Jesus because they answer his invitation and stay where he is. Similarly, Mary Magdalene's fidelity to Jesus is clear. She is healed by him and follows him, witnesses the crucifixion, comes to the tomb, and stays there. She doesn't understand but she remains.

After Mary hears Jesus call her name and recognizes him, Jesus says to her, "Do not hold on to me, because I have not yet ascended to the Father. But go to my brothers and say to them, 'I am ascending to my Father and your Father, to my

God and your God'" (John 20:17). This sentence is hard to understand, and many interpret it to mean that Mary has to stop holding on to the earthly Jesus in order to see the resurrected Christ. Some see in the statement a chronological time period in which resurrection appearances will end before Jesus ascends to the Father. In his commentary on John's Gospel, Raymond Brown states that this story about Mary Magdalene follows the story about the empty tomb, and in that story, it is stated clearly, "For they did not yet understand the scripture that he had to rise from the dead." Brown states that this appearance to Mary Magdalene is meant to clarify the meaning of resurrection. In John's Gospel, Jesus's death is already the beginning of his glorification. Death, resurrection, and ascension are of a piece, not separated chronologically but speaking of one movement.[11]

Jesus has already told the disciples that he has to go away to prepare a room for them and also that when he goes away, he will send the Holy Spirit to be God's presence with them (John 14—16). Jesus gives Mary Magdalene the meaning of that movement. He says, "I am ascending to my Father and your Father, to my God and your God." Brown points out that the statement Jesus makes to his disciples follows the same pattern as the statement Ruth makes to her mother-in-law, Naomi, in the book of Ruth.[12] Ruth and Naomi have been living in Moab because of a famine. They plan to travel back to Bethlehem in Judea when Ruth is notified that her husband has died. Because of this death, Ruth, who is a Moabite, has no obligation to travel with Naomi back to Judea. Naomi urges Ruth to stay behind, but Ruth replies, "Where you go, I will go; where you lodge, I will lodge; your people shall be my people, and your God my God" (Ruth 1:16). Ruth's statement is one of fidelity, kinship, and identity. Likewise, in John, Jesus's statement to Mary Magdalene is one of fidelity, kinship, and identity, intended not only for her but for all disciples of Jesus. The meaning of the one movement of Jesus's death, resurrection, and ascension is that Jesus's Father is our Father and his God our God. Furthermore, wherever we go, Christ's presence through the Holy Spirit will go with us. Our relationship to God and to others is in and through Jesus.[13] Mary is told to report what Jesus said "to my brothers." They are referred to as Jesus's brothers because they are now all a family, branches on the one, true vine, identified with Jesus as children of God, empowered to be children through the Holy Spirit. Mary has moved from darkness to light. In recognizing Jesus's voice, she has come home.

I think the creation symbolism that flows through this story, the mention of the first day of the week, the garden, and Mary mistaking Jesus as the gardener, is vital to understanding what is being said. In a book on Creation Theology in the Old Testament, Terrence Fretheim writes about the relationship of creation to redemption in the Book of Exodus: "The objective of God's work in redemption is to free people to be what they were created to be. This redemptive act is being delivered, not from the world but to true life in the world."[14] Similarly, in John's Gospel, Jesus says, "I came that they may have life, and have it abundantly" (John 10:10). Throughout the Bible, creation and redemption, creation and salvation are linked. We are saved so that we become children of God who participate in creation, even the creation of the truth of our identity.

In *New Seeds of Contemplation*, Merton writes,

> Our vocation is not simply to *be*, but to work together with God in the creation of our own life, our own identity, our own destiny. We are free beings and sons of God. This means to say that we should not passively exist, but actively participate

in His creative freedom, in our own lives, and the lives of others, by choosing the truth. To put it better, we are even called to share with God the work of *creating* the truth of our identity. We can evade this responsibility by playing with masks, and this pleases us because it can appear at times to be a free and creative way of living. It is quite easy, it seems to please everyone. But in the long run the cost and the sorrow come very high. To work out our own identity in God, which the Bible calls "working out our salvation," is a labor that requires sacrifice and anguish, risk and many tears. It demands close attention to reality at every moment, and great fidelity to God as He reveals Himself, obscurely, in the mystery of each new situation.[15]

Mary enters the garden of resurrection in mystery, mistakes Jesus for a gardener, and then calls him *Rabbouni*, teacher. Both gardeners and teachers tend to nature by giving nourishment and space for growth. Gardeners feed and water the plants, making sure there is enough space and rich soil for them to grow. Teachers recognize the gifts and challenges of their students and give them the tools they need to grow through challenges, to shape their own future, and to use their gifts to the best of their abilities. The best teachers and gardeners don't force or mold life to their will but allow growth to happen through participation. When we enter into Mary's experience in the garden of resurrection, we enter into that experience listening for the voice of Jesus that will awaken us to the truth of our identity and call us home. We know that listening for that voice comes in the midst of a world that often wants to misinterpret, distort, and explain away the truth that we know about ourselves and about God. The good news about the garden of resurrection is that in that garden our expectations are overturned and we are re-created, given the freedom to be children and participate with God in forming our identity, and working to bring God's kingdom to bear on the world. If we open ourselves to this transformation, we may find that our lives become far richer, far deeper, and far more abundant than we ever hoped they could be. We may find ourselves experiencing darkness with absolute trust in the irrepressible light of daybreak.

CHAPTER II

Prodigal Love

While he was at Bethany in the house of Simon the leper, as he sat at the table, a woman came with an alabaster jar of very costly ointment of nard, and she broke open the jar and poured the ointment on his head. But some were there who said to one another in anger, "Why was the ointment wasted in this way? For this ointment could have been sold for more than three hundred denarii, and the money given to the poor." And they scolded her. But Jesus said, "Let her alone; why do you trouble her? She has performed a good service for me. For you always have the poor with you, and you can show kindness to them whenever you wish; but you will not always have me. She has done what she could; she has anointed my body beforehand for its burial. Truly I tell you, wherever the good news is proclaimed in the whole world, what she has done will be told in remembrance of her."

Mark 14:3–9

My first pregnancy ended in a miscarriage. It was a sad and disappointing time. The joyful expectation of new life ended in death, and I felt like I had failed and was concerned that perhaps I would never experience what it was like to bring new life into the world. During this time, I had to have a procedure called a D and C. It is a common enough outpatient surgical procedure that is not terribly difficult physically but takes an emotional toll. I remember being in the hospital recovery room waking up from the procedure when a nurse came over with a warm blanket. With kindness and gentleness she laid the blanket over me and tucked it in all around me. I was so cold I was shaking and the warmth of that blanket, the weight of it, the gentle and kind way it was placed upon me was so soothing, so comforting. I remember the feeling of it to this day. The nurse had no personal connection to me. Covering me with that blanket was a routine task for her, and yet she did not perform it as a routine task. The gentleness and thoughtfulness behind her action tell me that she was in touch with compassion and found in her job a meaningful way to connect to others. I did not communicate with her at all, and so she had no way of knowing how profoundly her action touched me. I wonder how many patients she touched in this way, never knowing how meaningfully her kindness was received and felt.

I remember another time when a small kindness affected me deeply. I was in my forties and a failed friendship had left me feeling abandoned and alone. My children were leaving home for college; I was struggling to write my dissertation. It was a transition time for me, a time when I didn't quite know where I fit in the world. During this time I went to the library in town. I hadn't been to this particular library for some time, and the librarian remembered me from when my children were younger and I was a much more regular visitor. As she checked out my books, she expressed her joy at seeing me again, and told me how much she always enjoyed my former visits to the library and watching my children grow up. This small conversation moved me deeply, reaching beyond my dark lonely feelings of abandonment and touching the truth of my connections to many other people and many seasons of life.

These two personal experiences come to mind when I read the story of the unknown woman anointing Jesus on the head. The story comes at a dark time in Jesus's life. Before the story, we are told about the chief priests and scribes plotting to put Jesus to death, a time of darkness and suffering has already descended upon Jesus and he knows it. Immediately after the story, one of his own, a close friend and fellow worker for the kingdom, betrays him, handing him over to the authorities who are seeking to end his life. Between these stories of plotting and betrayal, a woman enters the home where Jesus is dining and pours an abundant quantity of perfumed oil over his head. The physical sensation of the oil, its dripping, its scent, and the thoughtfulness, kindness, and gentleness of the woman's actions move Jesus deeply. He is comforted by her action. He knows he has been understood.

The significance of her action becomes clearer when attention is paid to the unfolding of Jesus's story throughout Mark's Gospel. Three times in chapters 8—10, Jesus tells the disciples that he will have to suffer and die. The disciples are unable to listen to Jesus deeply enough to see clearly. They are blinded by their own ideas and hopes for the future. Peter knows Jesus is the Messiah, but his expectations of what the Messiah will be and do cannot contain the suffering and death Jesus speaks of. Jesus tells the disciples about carrying crosses, losing their lives for the sake of the kingdom, and being slaves of all. The disciples argue about who will be the greatest in the kingdom and about who will sit at the right and the left of Jesus. They don't understand. They can't see. One can only imagine that their lack of understanding and lack of sight left Jesus feeling quite alone. When the unknown woman anoints Jesus on the head, her actions break into his loneliness. One person has understood, has listened deeply enough to see, has grasped that he will suffer and die, has glimpsed the abundant love in his self-emptying suffering and death, and has expressed her gratitude and understanding in a reciprocal gesture of abundant love.

Jesus recognizes what she has done. He says several things about her action, "She has performed a good service for me….She has done what she could; she has anointed my body beforehand for its burial." Of all these statements, the claim that speaks most deeply to me is the claim that she has done what she could. The reason this speaks so profoundly to me is that it expresses a way in which we are all like this unknown woman. We are thrust into situations in which death overwhelms life, darkness overwhelms light, confusion overwhelms understanding, and we do what we can to show our love. Often, our loving actions are not enough to stop death from coming, are not enough to keep darkness from descending, and are sometimes not even perceived or understood by those we show our love to, but we do what we can.

My favorite relative when I was growing up was my Great Aunt Betty. Aunt Betty and her husband, Uncle Andy, lived across the state from us in Philadelphia but would come and visit us twice a year or so. Uncle Andy was my mother's uncle, my grandmother's brother. Aunt Betty was classy, gentle, and kind, but she was also spunky. I remember a minor incident from one of their visits when I was quite young, maybe six or seven years old. We were gathered around the dining room table eating dinner. We had all pretty much finished our dinners, but I had not eaten my broccoli. It was a vegetable I did not enjoy at the time. My mother looked around the table and told me to eat my broccoli. She then got lost in a conversation with someone else at the table. While my mother's attention lay elsewhere, Aunt Betty reached over, took the broccoli from my plate and fed it to our dog, Charlie. I was astonished! I never even thought about defying my mother and Aunt Betty's act of rebellion on my behalf was shocking, but I felt a deep comradery in it as well. I always felt that Aunt Betty was on my side, encouraging me to be myself and loving everything about me.

My Aunt Betty died of Alzheimer's disease when I was in my early thirties. At her funeral my Uncle Andy told me a story. In order to appreciate the story, you have to understand some of my uncle's characteristics. He was a rather difficult man. He had a habit of saying everything that was on his mind without regard for people's feelings. He was not a good listener and did not care to learn the concerns, needs, or desires of other people. He was also obsessive-compulsive and very demanding. He once told me that he had a method for rotating his socks so that every sock wore evenly. He also gave John and me some outdoor benches that were at least twenty-five years old. He gave them to us in their original boxes and on every box my uncle had drawn a diagram that explained how to put the benches back in the box at the end of summer so that they would not get weathered. I am afraid that those benches had a much shorter life in our house than they had in his. My uncle's obsession with benches, socks, and other material objects often kept him from meaningful connection to the people he loved.

The story my uncle told me the day of my aunt's funeral was a story about strawberries. My aunt lived in a nursing home for the last few years of her life. She no longer recognized the people she loved all the time, and like many Alzheimer's patients, she often talked of the past as though it were the present. Before she became sick with Alzheimer's, my Aunt Betty loved strawberries. When strawberry season came, she ate as many as she could and made strawberry jam, strawberry pie, and strawberry shortcake. When strawberry season came around the last year of my aunt's life, my Uncle Andy decided to give her a gift of strawberries. This was a much harder task for him than it sounds. He had to think about what she would like, what she would want. He had to go outside of his routine, make a trip to the grocery store, pick out the juiciest, ripest strawberries, bring them home, wash them, cut off the stems, put them in a container, and take them to my aunt in the nursing home. None of these tasks were part of his routine, none of them came easily or naturally for him, and all of them caused him stress. The stress he felt preparing the strawberries was palpable as he told me this story at my aunt's funeral. The story has an unfortunate ending. When my uncle offered the costly strawberries to my aunt, she turned her head away from them. For reasons we will never know, she refused his gift. My uncle concluded his story by saying, "All that effort was a waste."

The disciples of Jesus came to a similar conclusion when the unknown woman anointed Jesus on the head saying, "Why was the ointment wasted in this way?" But Jesus didn't think it was a waste. Jesus recognized it as the gift of abundant love that it was, a gift given in the midst of darkness. He received her gift as fully as he gave the gift of his own life. Mark tells us that Jesus looked at things differently than the rest of the world. Jesus saw the generosity and prodigal love in the two small coins a poor widow dropped in the temple treasury, and he saw the same generosity and prodigal love in the unknown woman's act of anointing. Jesus knew the power of prodigal love to overturn worlds, to heal broken hearts, and to create life in the midst of death. He perceived the generous widow who gave everything she had, her whole life, because he would give everything he had, his whole life. He heard in the actions of the unnamed anointing woman, her acceptance and understanding of his life. He knew she also understood the power of prodigal love to overturn worlds, to heal broken hearts, and to create life in the midst of death. While the disciples of Jesus heard "what a waste" when he told them that he would suffer and die, she understood. She understood that what looks like waste is often the most meaningful aspect of our lives.

When I had three young children and was attending Pittsburgh Theology Seminary, my days were filled with productivity. Oftentimes on my way home from a long day at the seminary, I would stop at the Giant Eagle in Ligonier late in the evening. Filled with efficient energy, I would quickly run into the store to get the few items I needed in order to check the last chore off my long list for the day. The store was fairly empty at that time of night, and I suspect for this reason, there was another mother who also shopped at this same time. I didn't know this mother, never spoke to her. She was always with her son who had a disability. Her son had difficulty walking and controlling his body. His movements were chaotic and painfully slow, but his mother would calmly, gently, and quietly place his hands on the handle of the shopping cart and help him to walk and push the cart. She would talk softly with him and consult him about purchases. Her son's disability shaped her life. She lived on the margins; shopped when no one else did, experienced life at an exasperatingly slow pace, a pace that would frustrate most of us, a pace we might even consider a waste of time. As I passed them by with my lists, my busyness, and my efficient, productive energy, I knew a truth I could not quite express, the truth that in this field of prodigal love between mother and disabled son lay buried treasure.

Similarly, my uncle's story about strawberries is a lesson about deeper truth. It is a lesson about giving in the most trying of circumstances, loving when there is no reward, digging more deeply into patience than you ever thought possible, and finding that it is in this giving, loving, and digging deeply that you find the pearl of great price. These actions are the actions of discipleship, and when we find a way to love prodigally in the midst of darkness, we respond to Jesus's extravagant gesture of love, Jesus's willing entry into vulnerability, broken, given, and poured out for us. My uncle's story of strawberries revealed that lying buried in his obsessive-compulsive behavior, hidden behind his concern with socks and benches, beyond concerns that often prevented him from connecting with others, lay an abiding love for my aunt that was his deepest truth. With a prodigal gift of strawberries, he did what he could.

The story about the unknown woman who anoints Jesus ends with Jesus's proclamation, "Truly I tell you, wherever the good news is proclaimed in the whole world, what she has done will be told in remembrance of her" (Mark 14:9). It is an interesting statement because on a historical level, it isn't true; her forgotten name is a casualty of the neglected history of women. Yet on a poetic level, the statement rings true. Her memory lives on when the gospel is proclaimed by a nurse in the hospital who offers a warm blanket to a sad patient, by a librarian who comforts a lonely woman with kindness, by a mother who patiently cares for her disabled son, and by a man who, though bound by an obsessive-compulsive disorder, reaches beyond himself to offer his dying wife strawberries. The unknown woman lives in each one of us who finds a way to let the irrepressible light that darkness cannot overcome shape our actions so that, reaching for prodigal love, we proclaim the gospel by doing what we can.

> Truly I tell you, just as you did it to one of the least of these who are members of my family, you did it to me. (Matt 25:40)

CONCLUSION

The Beauty of Irises

In a masterful book on the Christian practice of contemplation, *Into the Silent Land*, Martin Laird tells the story of a woman, Elizabeth. Elizabeth suffers with an autoimmune disease that causes her severe pain and keeps her confined to bed. In her suffering, she turns to the practice of contemplative prayer. While Elizabeth's prayer practice does not take away her pain or heal her disease, it does help her to experience God's presence in the midst of her suffering. She finds a silent center to her pain, a silence in which she experiences both communion with God and communion with others. Pain no longer isolates her from other people. Her attentiveness to prayer leads her to self-forgetful, loving attentiveness to every person that helps her or comes to visit her as her illness continues. People who come to help her find instead that they are the recipients of Elizabeth's deep listening, healing presence.[1]

Elizabeth was an academic botanist and one of the world's authorities on irises. Her illness put a halt to her research, her lab work, her scientific reports about rhizomes, but she claimed that from her bed, through her suffering she had learned something new about irises. Laird writes,

The Beauty of Irises

Not long before Elizabeth died she was talking about how she missed her life as a botanist, about the unfinished projects that would remain unfinished. She said, "You know, while I've been ill I have managed to discover something new about irises—I never knew they were beautiful."[2]

I share this story with you at the conclusion of this study of women in the New Testament because though I have not been ill, have not been suffering, if I were to try to describe the effect writing this study has had on my life, Elizabeth's discovery of the beauty of irises is as close as I can get to expressing the joy of discovery I have had through all aspects of this project.

I have been engaged in an academic study of the Bible for twenty years. Without that academic study, this book would not be possible, and yet learning to let go of academic expectations, allowing myself to write from the perspective of exploration rather than obligation has opened for me pathways of discovery I never knew before. These pathways have led me to discover the beauty I have experienced in my own life, beauty that has existed even in the painful moments of my life. These pathways have led me to feel more deeply connected to the deep healing presence of God who has accompanied me throughout my journey and given me countless gifts. These pathways have helped me to feel less isolated, to feel a deep connection to others as I share my own story knowing that within the particularities of that story is a shared human experience of the joys, sorrows, ambiguities, and love that make every life valuable and connected to all other lives.

It has been some time since I began this writing project. At that time, I knew I could not write about every woman in the New Testament and so I selected those I felt most compelled to write about. It is interesting to think that if I were going to begin this book today, I might choose different women to write about and even were I to write about the same women, I would likely choose different themes to explore, not because the choices I made were wrong but simply because the experiences of my life are different than they were a few years ago. This is a testimony to the richness of the biblical text. Its beauty and compelling power are never exhausted. We can live in the Bible, turning it over and over, growing old and gray in it.[3]

I am grateful for the witness of the women in the New Testament. I have learned so much from them about living a faithful life. We usually read the gospel from the perspective of the men with a focus on the political, social, and visible pronouncements of Jesus's message. When we shift our attention to the women, we shift our focus to the hidden, the unexplored, the small everyday matters of daily life, and through this shift in our focus the biblical text is rounded out and we awaken to the wholeness of life that Jesus engages and seeks to transform. These women teach us that no matter where we are in our lives, whether we are joyful or sorrowful, experience blessing or grief, whether we have status and a firm place in society or are experiencing isolation and a sense of inadequacy, we all share a common power, the power to turn to God in prayer, to enter into the deep spaces and open our hearts to God, to catch a glimpse of the irrepressible light deep within.

I have a framed painting that hangs above the desk in my office. This painting was given to me by a dear friend I met while attending Pittsburgh Theological Seminary. It is a depiction of Mother Teresa of Calcutta hugging an obviously poor, abandoned little girl with large, soulful eyes. A quote attributed to Mother Teresa appears in the painting. It says, "To show great love for God and our neighbor, we need not do great things. It is how much love we put in the doing that makes our offering something beautiful for God." The women of the New Testament teach us to see the beauty in the small, ordinary, everyday moments of our lives. If we offer all of these moments to God with great love for God and our neighbor, our offering will be something beautiful for God.

Notes

PREFACE

1. This saying was discussed in our class because it was quoted in a chapter about how Jews and Christians read the Bible. Amy Grossblat Pessah, Kenneth J. Meyers, and Christopher M. Leighton, "How Do Jews and Christians Read the Bible?" *Irreconcilable Differences? A Learning Resource for Jews and Christians*, ed. David F. Sandmel, Rosann M. Catalano, and Christopher M. Leighton (Boulder, CO: Westview Press, 2001), 59.

CHAPTER I

1. Karl Rahner, "Thoughts on the Theology of Christmas," in *Theological Investigations*, vol. 3, trans. Karl H. and Boniface Kruger (Baltimore: Helicon, 1967), 24–28.

2. Donald E. Gowan, "Wealth and Poverty in the Old Testament: The Case of the Widow, the Orphan, and the Sojourner," *Interpretation* (October 1987): 341.

3. R. T. France, *The Gospel of Mark: A Commentary on the Greek Text* (Grand Rapids: Eerdmans, 2002), 491.

4. Thomas Merton, *Hagia Sophia* (Lexington: Stamperia del Santuccio, 1962); here extracted from *The Collected Poems of Thomas Merton* (New York: New Directions, 1977), 370–71.

CHAPTER 2

1. It is unclear whether Anna was eighty-four years old or had been a widow for eighty-four years. See Bonnie Thurston, "Who Was Anna? Luke 2:36–38," *Perspectives in Religious Studies* 28, no. 1 (Spring 2001): 49.

2. Andrés García Serrano, "Anna's Characterization in Luke 2:36–38: A Case of Conceptual Allusion?," *Catholic Biblical Quarterly* 76, no. 3 (July 2014): 468.

3. For a discussion of the role of women in the Gospel of Luke, see Jane Schaberg, "Luke," in *The Women's Bible Commentary*, ed. Carol A. Newsom and Sharon H. Ringe (Louisville: Westminster/John Knox Press, 1992), 275–92.

4. Serrano, "Anna's Characterization in Luke 2:36–38," 464.

5. Thurston, "Who Was Anna?," 49; Serrano, "Anna's Characterization in Luke 2:36–38," 468.

6. Serrano, "Anna's Characterization in Luke 2:36–38," 468.

CHAPTER 3

1. Donald E. Gowan, *Theology in Exodus: Biblical Theology in the Form of a Commentary* (Louisville: Westminster John Knox Press, 1994), 200; Elizabeth A. Johnson, *She Who Is: The Mystery of God in Feminist Theological Discourse* (New York: Crossroad, 2000), 85.

2. Johnson, *She Who Is*, 85.

3. Johnson, *She Who Is*, 85–86.

4. Gowan, *Theology in Exodus*, 200–202; Johnson, *She Who Is*, 85–86.

5. Margaret Wise Brown, *The Runaway Bunny Revised Edition* (New York: HarperCollins, 2006).

6. Hans Urs Von Balthasar, *Theo Drama: Theological Dramatic Theory, vol. 5; The Last Act* (San Francisco: Ignatius Press, 2003), 74–146.

CHAPTER 4

1. Leonardo Boff, *Trinity and Society*, trans. Paul Burns (Eugene, Oregon: Wipf and Stock, 1988), 217.

2. Frances Taylor Gench, *Back to the Well: Women's Encounters with Jesus in the Gospels* (Louisville: Westminster John Knox Press, 2004), 29.

3. *The Jewish Annotated New Testament: New Revised Standard Version Bible Translation*, eds. Amy-Jill Levine and Marc Zvi Brettler (New York: Oxford University Press, 2011), 70.

4. Elisabeth Moltmann-Wendel, *I Am My Body: A Theology of Embodiment* (New York: Continuum, 1995), ix.

5. An example of this can be seen in Ben Witherington, *Women in the Ministry of Jesus: A Study of Jesus' Attitudes to Women and Their Roles as Reflected in His Earthly-Life* (Cambridge: Cambridge University Press, 1984), 73; For more examples, see note 20 in Frances Taylor Gench, *Back to the Well*, 35.

6. Victor Hugo, *Les Misérables*, trans. Charles E. Wilbour (New York: The Modern Library, 1992), 163.

7. Jürgen Moltmann, "Lived Theology: An Intellectual Biography," *The Asbury Theological Journal* 55, no. 1 (Spring 2000): 9–11.

CHAPTER 5

1. Walter T. Wilson, "The Uninvited Healer: Houses, Healing and Prophets in Matthew 8:1–22," *Journal for the Study of the New Testament* 36, no. 1 (2014): 58–59.

2. John R. Donahue and Daniel J. Harrington, *The Gospel of Mark* (Collegeville, MN: Liturgical Press, 2002), 81; Stephen J. Binz, *Peter: Fisherman and Shepherd of the Church* (Grand Rapids: Brazos Press, 2011), 20–21.

3. Donahue and Harrington, *Mark*, 82.

4. Donahue and Harrington, *Mark*, 82.

5. Bonnie Bowman Thurston, *Preaching Mark* (Minneapolis: Fortress Press, 2002), 28.

6. Binz, *Peter*, 20.

7. Binz, *Peter*, 20; W. D. Davies and Dale C. Allison Jr., *The Gospel according to Saint Matthew*, vol. 2 (Edinburgh: T&T Clark, 1991), 33–34.

8. Mary Ann Tolbert, "Mark," in *The Women's Bible Commentary*, ed. Carol A. Newsom and Sharon H. Ringe (Louisville, KY: Westminster John Knox Press, 1992), 267.

9. Thurston, *Preaching Mark*, 22.

10. Esther de Waal, *Seeking God: The Way of St. Benedict* (Collegeville, MN: Liturgical Press, 1984), 55.

11. Joan Chittister, *Wisdom Distilled from the Daily: Living the Rule of St. Benedict Today* (New York: HarperCollins, 1990), 51–52.

CHAPTER 6

1. Poling Sun, "Naming the Dog: Another Asian Reading of Mark 7:24–30," *Review and Expositor* 107 (Summer 2010): 388–89.

2. Sun, "Naming the Dog," 388–89.

3. John R. Donahue and Daniel J. Harrington, *The Gospel of Mark*, ed. Daniel J. Harrington (Collegeville, MN: Liturgical Press, 2002), 232.

4. Sun, "Naming the Dog," 389.

5. Jim Perkinson, "A Canaanitic Word in the Logos of Christ; or the Difference the Syro-Phoenician Woman Makes to Jesus," *Semeia* 75 (1996): 65–67.

6. The following discussion is informed by Sobrino's discussion of the historical unfolding of Jesus's faith in Jon Sobrino, *Christology at the Crossroads*, trans. John Drury (Eugene, OR: Wipf and Stock, 1978), 79–145.

7. Bonnie Thurston, *Women in the New Testament* (New York: Crossroad, 1998), 72.

8. William Barclay, *The Gospel of Mark*, 2nd ed., Daily Study Bible (Philadelphia: Westminster, 1956), 2:122, quoted in Sun, "Naming the Dog," 382.

9. A more complete list of controversies can be found in Daniel C. Harlow, "Early Judaism and Early Christianity," in *Early*

Judaism: A Comprehensive Overview, ed. John J. Collins and Daniel C. Harlow (Grand Rapids: Eerdmans, 2012), 394.

10. Bonnie Bowman Thurston, *Preaching Mark* (Minneapolis: Fortress Press, 2002), 88; W. D. Davies and Dale C. Allison Jr., *The International Critical Commentary on the Gospel according to Matthew*, vol. 2, (Edinburgh: T&T Clark, 1991), 551–56.

11. Eric Metaxas, *Bonhoeffer: Pastor, Martyr, Prophet, Spy* (Nashville: Thomas Nelson, 2010), 528.

12. Metaxas, *Bonhoeffer*, 528.

13. Dietrich Bonhoeffer, *Letters and Papers from Prison*, ed. Eberhard Bethge (New York: Touchstone, 1997), 347–48.

14. I listened to a recording of this sermon as part of a homiletics course I took when I attended Pittsburgh Theological Seminary from 1995 to 1999. My description of the sermon is from memory and may not be an accurate portrayal of the sermon.

CHAPTER 7

1. I read this story in James Martin, *The Jesuit Guide to Almost Everything: A Spirituality for Real Life* (New York: Harper Collins, 2012), 211–12.

2. John Nolland, *Word Biblical Commentary Volume 35 B, Luke 9:21—18:34* (Nashville: Thomas Nelson, 1993), 598–606.

3. Demetrius Dumm, "Benedictine Hospitality," *Benedictines* 35, no. 1 (Spring–Summer): 64–75; Henri J. M. Nouwen, "Hospitality," in *Monastic Studies* 10 (1974): 7–9.

4. Frances Taylor Gench, *Back to the Well: Women's Encounters with Jesus in the Gospels* (Louisville: Westminster John Knox Press, 2004), 56–57.

5. Gench, *Back to the Well*, 56–57; Loveday C. Alexander, "Sisters in Adversity: Retelling Martha's Story," in *A Feminist Companion to Luke*, ed. Amy-Jill Levine with Marianne Blickenstaff (Cleveland: Pilgrim Press, 2001), 197–98.

6. Alexander, "Sisters in Adversity," 197–213.

7. Alexander, "Sisters in Adversity," 206.

8. Alexander, "Sisters in Adversity," 206.

9. Bonnie Thurston, *Women in the New Testament* (New York: Crossroad, 1998), 107–11.

10. Terrence Kardong, "To Receive All as Christ," *Cistercian Studies* 19, no. 3 (1984): 195.

11. Kardong, "To Receive All," 197–98.

12. Dumm, "Benedictine Hospitality," 70–71.

13. Dumm, "Benedictine Hospitality," 70–71.

14. Dumm, "Benedictine Hospitality," 65–67.

15. Nouwen, "Hospitality," 2.

16. Thomas Merton, *New Seeds of Contemplation* (New York: New Directions, 2007), 32–33.

17. Thomas Merton, *Woods, Shore, Desert: A Notebook May 1968* (Santa Fe: Museum of New Mexico Press, 1982), 48.

CHAPTER 8

1. Sandra M. Schneiders, *The Revelatory Text: Interpreting the New Testament as Sacred Scripture* (Collegeville, MN: Liturgical Press, 1999), 188–94.

2. John A. Sanford, *Mystical Christianity: A Psychological Commentary on the Gospel of John* (New York: Crossroad, 1993), 4.

3. Demetrius R. Dumm, *A Mystical Portrait of Jesus* (Collegeville, MN: Liturgical Press, 2001), viii.

4. Schneiders, *Revelatory Text*, 188–94.

5. Craig R. Koester, *Symbolism in the Fourth Gospel: Meaning, Mystery, Community* (Minneapolis: Fortress Press, 1995), 155.

6. Koester, *Symbolism*, 167–81.

7. L. William Countryman, *The Mystical Way in the Fourth Gospel: Crossing Over into God* (Harrisburg, PA: Trinity Press International, 1994), 32–49; Dumm, *Mystical Portrait*, 99–100.

8. Koester, *Symbolism*, 168.

CHAPTER 9

1. Paige Montrose, a student in the honors program at St. Vincent College, generously agreed to allow me to use her answer in this chapter.

2. W. D. Davies and Dale C. Allison Jr., *The International Critical Commentary on the Gospel according to Matthew* 3 vols. (Edinburgh: T&T Clark, 1991), 1:209.

3. Donald E. Gowan, "Salvation as Healing," *Ex Auditu* 5 (1989): 2.

4. Davies and Allison, *ICC Matthew*, 3:472–474.

5. *Rule of Benedict in English*, ed. Timothy Fry, OSB, chap. 4.

6. Frederick Buechner, *Secrets in the Dark: A Life in Sermons* (New York: Harper One, 1973), 19.

7. This paragraph was influenced by Gerald May, "Entering the Emptiness," in *Simple Living, Compassionate Life: A Christian Perspective*, ed. Michael Schut (Denver, CO: Living the Good News, 1999), 41–51.

CHAPTER 10

1. Mary Ann Getty-Sullivan, *Women in the New Testament* (Collegeville, MN: The Liturgical Press, 2001), 191.

2. Getty-Sullivan, *Women in the New Testament*, 184.

3. Getty-Sullivan, *Women in the New Testament*, 183.

4. Elizabeth Moltmann-Wendel, *The Women around Jesus*, trans. John Bowden (New York: Crossroad, 1982), 61–67.

5. Robin Griffith-Jones, *Beloved Disciple: The Misunderstood Legacy of Mary Magdalene, the Woman Closest to Jesus* (New York: Harper One, 2008), xii.

6. Moltmann-Wendel, *Women around Jesus*, 64–67.

7. My thoughts about connecting this passage to the importance of women's reputations came from reading Carla Ricci, *Mary*

Magdalene and Many Others: Women Who Followed Jesus, trans. Paul Burns (Minneapolis: Fortress Press, 1994), 135–36.

8. Ricci, *Mary Magdalene and Many Others,* 135–56.

9. Griffith-Jones, *Beloved Disciple,* 23.

10. Griffith-Jones, *Beloved Disciple,* 35–36.

11. Raymond E. Brown, *The Gospel according to John XIII–XXI* (New York: Doubleday, 1970), 1013–17.

12. Brown, *The Gospel according to John XIII–XXI,* 1016.

13. Brown, *The Gospel according to John XIII–XXI,* 1016.

14. Terrence E. Fretheim, *God and World in the Old Testament: A Relational Theology of Creation* (Nashville: Abingdon Press, 2005), 125.

15. Thomas Merton, *New Seeds of Contemplation* (New York: New Directions, 1961), 32.

CONCLUSION

1. Martin Laird, *Into the Silent Land: A Guide to the Christian Practice of Contemplation* (New York: Oxford University Press, 2006), 107–10.

2. Laird, *Into the Silent Land,* 110.

3. This is drawn from a saying quoted in full in the introduction. The full statement can be found in Amy Grossblat Pessah, Kenneth J. Meyers, and Christopher M. Leighton, "How Do Jews and Christians Read the Bible?," *Irreconcilable Differences? A Learning Resource for Jews and Christians,* ed. David F. Sandmel, Rosann M. Catalano, and Christopher M. Leighton (Boulder, CO: Westview Press, 2001), 59.